AIRBOY

WRITTEN BY
JAMES ROBINSON

ART & LETTERING BY
GREG HINKLE

EDITED BY

JOEL ENOS
JAMIE S. RICH

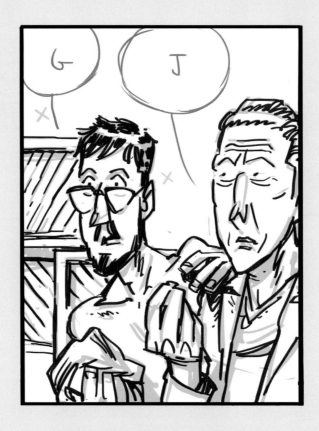

AIRBOY DELUXE HC. APRIL 2016.
FIRST PRINTING
ISBN: 978-1-63215-543-6

PUBLISHED BY IMAGE COMICS, INC.
OFFICE OF PUBLICATION: 2001 CENTER STREET, 6TH FLOOR, BERKELEY, CA 94704. COPYRIGHT © 2016
JAMES ROBINSON & GREG HINKLE. ALL RIGHTS RESERVED. GOLDEN AGE AIRBOY AND CHARACTERS
CREATED FOR HILLMAN PERIODICALS BY CHARLES BIRO, DICK WOOD, & AL CAMY. AIRBOY™ (INCLUDING
ALL PROMINENT CHARACTERS FEATURED HEREIN), ITS LOGO AND ALL CHARACTER LIKENESSES ARE
TRADEMARKS OF JAMES ROBINSON & GREG HINKLE UNLESS OTHERWISE NOTED.
ORIGINALLY PUBLISHED IN SINGLE MAGAZINE FORM AS AIRBOY #1-4.

FOR INFORMATION REGARDING THE CPSIA ON THIS PRINTED MATERIAL
CALL: 203-595-3636 AND PROVIDE REFERENCE # RICH -- 668301.
FOR INTERNATIONAL RIGHTS, CONTACT: FOREIGNLICENSING@IMAGECOMICS.COM

I GOT THE IDEA FOR *AIRBOY* AT A PIVOTAL JUNCTURE IN MY LIFE. MY WIFE AND I HAD BEGUN A SEPARATION, AND WERE STARTING THE PROCESS OF ACTUALLY BREAKING UP. AT THE SAME TIME, HITTING MY NADIR IN TERMS OF ALCOHOL CONSUMPTION, I HAD DECIDED IT WAS TIME TO BURY THE BOTTLE INSTEAD OF DOWNING IT, AND TO SOBER UP FOR GOOD. I HAD ALSO LEFT BEHIND SOME UNPLEASANT AND SOUL-DESTROYING WORKING EXPERIENCES AND WAS BEGINNING TO FEEL REINVIGORATED CREATIVELY. IT WAS VERY MUCH A TIME OF CHANGE.

ALTHOUGH I CAN MORE OR LESS PINPOINT THE TIME WHEN I FIRST DREAMED UP THE SEED THAT WOULD BECOME *AIRBOY*, IN ALL HONESTLY I DON'T KNOW HOW THE IDEA FIRST TOOK SHAPE. I RECALL THE MOVIE *ADAPTATION* WAS IN MY MIND AT THE TIME, AND THE WORK OF HUNTER S. THOMPSON. ALSO THE IDEA OF TELLING THE TRUTH, ALBEIT THROUGH THE WARPED LENS OF SATIRE. A HUGE INFLUENCE ALSO WAS CHESTER BROWN'S AUTOBIOGRAPHIC GRAPHIC NOVEL, *PAYING FOR IT*, WHICH CHRONICLED HIS DEALINGS WITH PROSTITUTES AND THE EMOTIONAL JOURNEY HE WENT THROUGH ALONG THE WAY. IT'S A WORK THAT DESERVES A WIDER AUDIENCE. I THINK IT'S BRILLIANT. AND AS FAR AS IT INSPIRED WHAT I DID IN *AIRBOY*, I THINK WHAT IMPRESSED ME MOST ABOUT *PAYING FOR IT*, AND WHAT I HOPED TO ACHIEVE MYSELF, WAS THE MIXTURE OF UTTER CANDOR AND HEART AND EMOTION THAT HE CAPTURED SO BEAUTIFULLY.

BUT OF COURSE CHESTER WASN'T RUNNING AROUND THE STREETS OF SAN FRANCISCO WITH HIS PANTS OFF, ENGAGING IN AN ADVENTURE WITH A GOLDEN AGE COMIC BOOK AVIATION HERO. NO, THAT WAS ALL ME.

I HAD STARTED OUT -- A MILLION YEARS AGO -- WHILE WAITING TO GET IN AS A WRITER AT THE BIG TWO, MARVEL AND DC COMICS, BY WRITING ODD LITTLE GRAPHIC NOVELS AND MINI-SERIES FOR SMALLER COMPANIES. DOES ANYONE FAMILIAR WITH MY WORK RECALL *ILLEGAL ALIEN*, *BLUE BEARD*, *67 SECONDS* AND MY FIRST PUBLISHED WORK *LONDON'S DARK*? I HAD NEVER MEANT TO STEP AWAY FROM DOING THINGS THAT WERE MORE PERSONAL AND EXPERIMENTAL, AND YET IT HAD BEEN YEARS SINCE I'VE EVEN THOUGHT OF DOING ANYTHING LIKE THAT. YEARS? NO, THINKING ABOUT IT, IT'S BEEN DECADES.

I WANTED TO SCRAPE THE CREATIVE RUST FROM ME AND I THOUGHT *AIRBOY* WOULD BE JUST THE THING TO DO THAT. I WANTED TO PUSH THE BOUNDARIES. I WANTED TO SHOCK AND PROVOKE. I WANTED TO CONVEY ALL THE FEARS AND INSECURITIES GOING ON INSIDE ME -- THE PETTY CREATIVE JEALOUSIES, THE DREAD SINKING FEAR THAT THE NEXT IDEA IN MY HEAD WOULD BE THE LAST I'D EVER HAVE. I WANTED TO STRIP MYSELF BARE. AND I WANTED TO DO IT WITH HUMOR THAT MADE ME THE PUNCH LINE AS MUCH AS POSSIBLE.

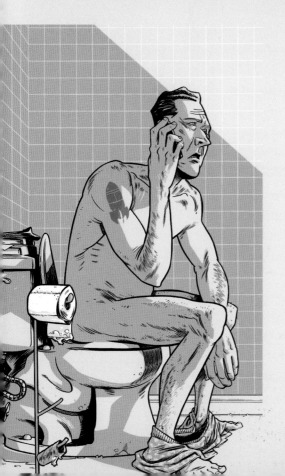

I WAS BORN LUCKY AND THAT LUCK WAS CERTAINLY IN PLAY THE DAY I MET GREG HINKLE. WE WERE BOTH LIVING IN SAN FRANCISCO AT THAT TIME AND I WAS IMMEDIATELY TAKEN WITH HIS ART. I THEN SAW THE WORK HE AND WRITER JASON MCNAMARA WERE DOING ON THEIR GRAPHIC NOVEL *THE RATTLER* AND I WAS DOUBLY IMPRESSED. I SUGGESTED WE WORK TOGETHER AND TOLD HIM THE IDEA I HAD -- BOTH OF US IN THE BOOK, THE NUDITY, THE DRUGS, THE OUTLANDISH ALMOST MONSTROUS VERSIONS OF OURSELVES -- AND HE SIGNED ON. I WILL ALWAYS BE GRATEFUL TO GREG FOR BEING A PART OF SUCH A CRAZY VENTURE, AT SUCH AN EARLY JUNCTURE IN HIS CAREER.

MY OTHER DEBT OF GRATITUDE GOES TO MY EX-WIFE JANN. AS I SAID ABOVE, WHEN THE IDEA FOR *AIRBOY* FIRST OCCURRED TO ME, WE WERE SEPARATED BUT STILL WORKING ON OUR RELATIONSHIP. I TOLD HER WHAT I HAD IN MIND AND HOW IT WOULD SHOW OUR RELATIONSHIP AND MY FAILINGS WITHIN IT. ALSO THE FACT THAT SHE'D BE FEATURED IN THE BOOK TO A SMALL DEGREE. SHE AGREED, UNDERSTANDING THE SPOTLIGHT SHE MIGHT BE UNDER, BUT SUPPORTING MY WORK NONE-THE-LESS. AND FOR THAT, ALONG WITH HER CONTINUED FRIENDSHIP TO THIS DAY, I WILL NEVER BE ABLE TO THANK HER ENOUGH.

AND THERE YOU ARE. *AIRBOY*. A WORK THAT HAS DELIGHTED SOME AND ANGERED OTHERS. CERTAINLY PROVOCATIVE. HOPEFULLY FUNNY. BUT MORE SO, HOPEFULLY...IN ITS OWN WARPED WAY, SINCERE.

- JAMES ROBINSON

IMAGE COMICS, INC.
ROBERT KIRKMAN - CHIEF OPERATING OFFICER
ERIK LARSEN - CHIEF FINANCIAL OFFICER
TODD MCFARLANE - PRESIDENT
MARC SILVESTRI - CHIEF EXECUTIVE OFFICER
JIM VALENTINO - VICE-PRESIDENT
ERIC STEPHENSON - PUBLISHER
COREY MURPHY - DIRECTOR OF SALES
JEFF BOISON - DIRECTOR OF PUBLISHING PLANNING & BOOK TRADE SALES
JEREMY SULLIVAN - DIRECTOR OF DIGITAL SALES
KAT SALAZAR - DIRECTOR OF PR & MARKETING
EMILY MILLER - DIRECTOR OF OPERATIONS
BRANWYN BIGGLESTONE - SENIOR ACCOUNTS MANAGER
SARAH MELLO - ACCOUNTS MANAGER
DREW GILL - ART DIRECTOR
JONATHAN CHAN - PRODUCTION MANAGER
MEREDITH WALLACE - PRINT MANAGER
BRIAH SKELLY - PUBLICITY ASSISTANT
SASHA HEAD - SALES & MARKETING PRODUCTION DESIGNER
RANDY OKAMURA - DIGITAL PRODUCTION DESIGNER
DAVID BROTHERS - BRANDING MANAGER
ALLY POWER - CONTENT MANAGER
ADDISON DUKE - PRODUCTION ARTIST
VINCENT KUKUA - PRODUCTION ARTIST
TRICIA RAMOS - PRODUCTION ARTIST
JEFF STANG - DIRECT MARKET SALES REPRESENTATIVE
EMILIO BAUTISTA - DIGITAL SALES ASSOCIATE
LEANNA CAUNTER - ACCOUNTING ASSISTANT
CHLOE RAMOS-PETERSON - ADMINISTRATIVE ASSISTANT
IMAGECOMICS.COM

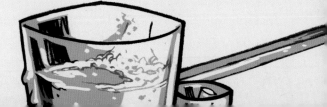

CHAPTER 1

AIRBOY

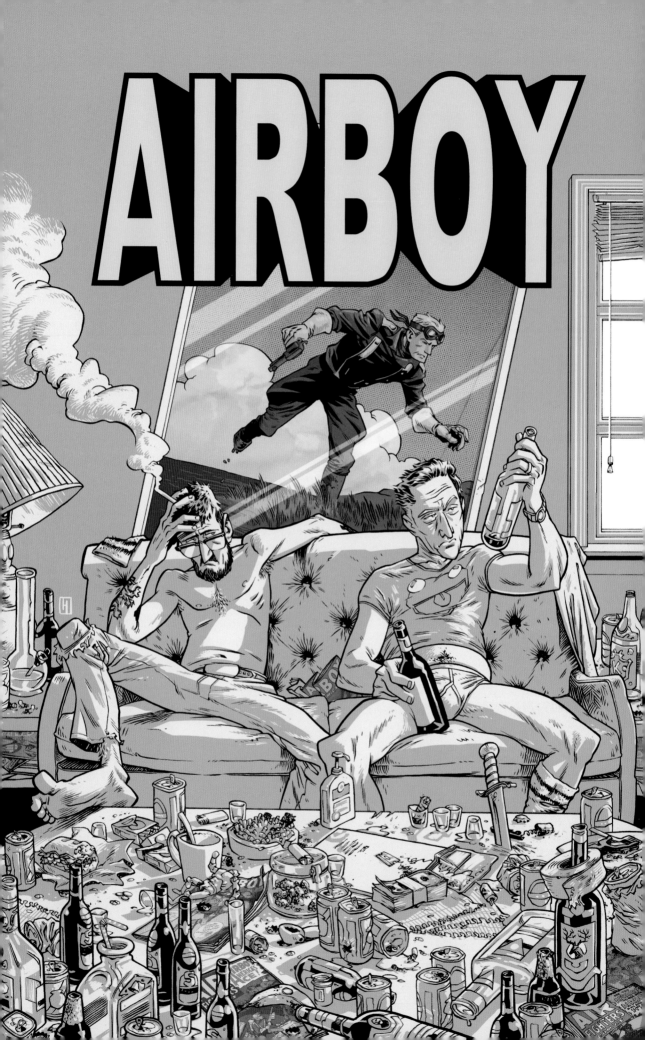

JAMES ROBINSON
NO, ERIC, NO WAY...
I FUCKING HATE AIRBOY.

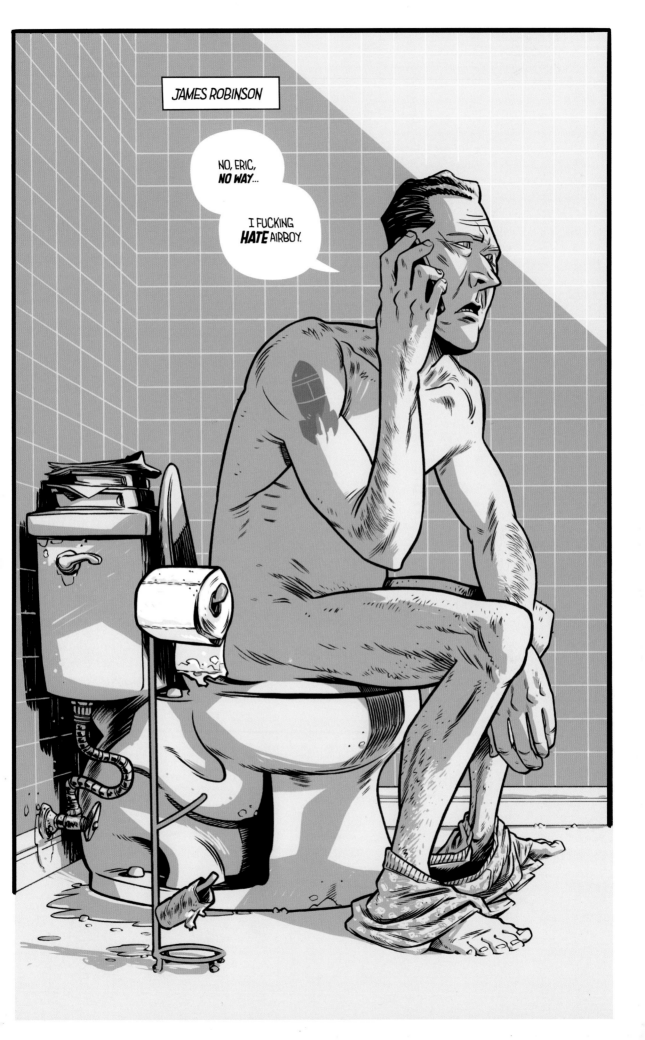

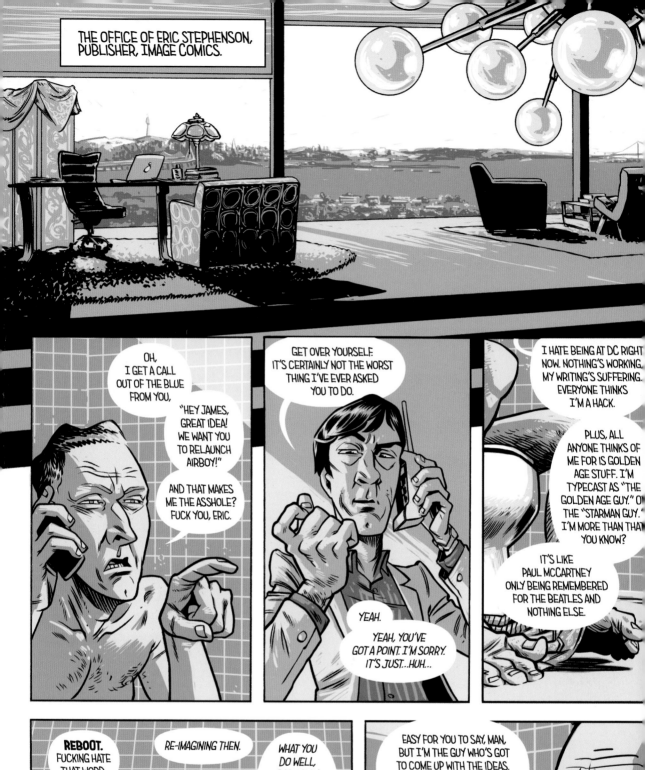

THE OFFICE OF ERIC STEPHENSON, PUBLISHER, IMAGE COMICS.

OH, I GET A CALL OUT OF THE BLUE FROM YOU,

"HEY JAMES, GREAT IDEA! WE WANT YOU TO RELAUNCH AIRBOY!"

AND THAT MAKES ME THE ASSHOLE? FUCK YOU, ERIC.

GET OVER YOURSELF. IT'S CERTAINLY NOT THE WORST THING I'VE EVER ASKED YOU TO DO.

YEAH. YEAH, YOU'VE GOT A POINT. I'M SORRY. IT'S JUST...HUH...

I HATE BEING AT DC RIGHT NOW. NOTHING'S WORKING. MY WRITING'S SUFFERING. EVERYONE THINKS I'M A HACK.

PLUS, ALL ANYONE THINKS OF ME FOR IS GOLDEN AGE STUFF. I'M TYPECAST AS "THE GOLDEN AGE GUY." OR THE "STARMAN GUY." I'M MORE THAN THAT, YOU KNOW?

IT'S LIKE PAUL MCCARTNEY ONLY BEING REMEMBERED FOR THE BEATLES AND NOTHING ELSE.

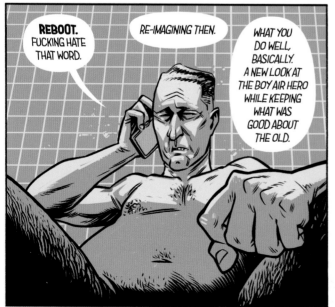

REBOOT. FUCKING HATE THAT WORD.

RE-IMAGINING THEN.

WHAT YOU DO WELL, BASICALLY. A NEW LOOK AT THE BOY AIR HERO WHILE KEEPING WHAT WAS GOOD ABOUT THE OLD.

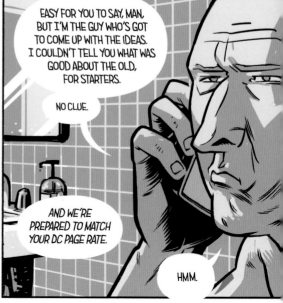

EASY FOR YOU TO SAY, MAN, BUT I'M THE GUY WHO'S GOT TO COME UP WITH THE IDEAS. I COULDN'T TELL YOU WHAT WAS GOOD ABOUT THE OLD, FOR STARTERS.

NO CLUE.

AND WE'RE PREPARED TO MATCH YOUR DC PAGE RATE.

HMM.

JUST CONSIDER IT, I THINK THAT'S A REASONABLE ENOUGH THING TO ASK YOU.
DON'T BE AN ASSHOLE.
I DON'T BELIEVE IT.
THAT PEOPLE ONLY REMEMBER ME FOR STARMAN?
NO, THAT YOU JUST COMPARED YOURSELF TO PAUL MCCARTNEY.
CULLY HAMNER'S RIGHT ABOUT YOU, YOU'RE AN **EGOMANIAC**.
CULLY SAID THAT?
OR TONY HARRIS.
ONE OF THOSE GUYS.
LOOK, PAUL, JUST THINK ABOUT IT, OKAY? I GOT A COUPLE OF OTHER GUYS IN MIND IF YOU SAY NO, BUT I'M COMING TO YOU FIRST.
AIRBOY IS IN PUBLIC DOMAIN AND HE'S SORT OF FORGOTTEN BUT WITH A NAME THAT EVERYONE REMEMBERS. HE'D BE GREAT FOR A REBOOT.
I'M A BIT BLOCKED.
THEN GO TO A MUSEUM, A MOVIE-- LISTEN TO SOME MUSIC. YOU'LL START WRITING AGAIN BEFORE YOU KNOW IT.
NOT WHAT I MEANT, BUT DULY NOTED.

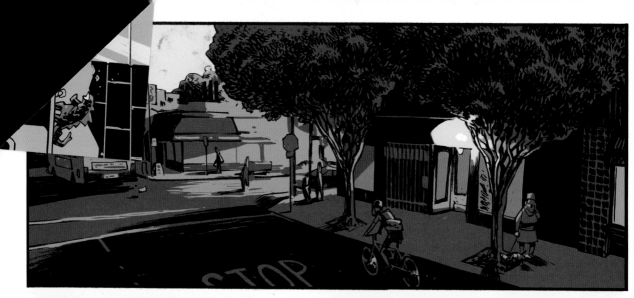

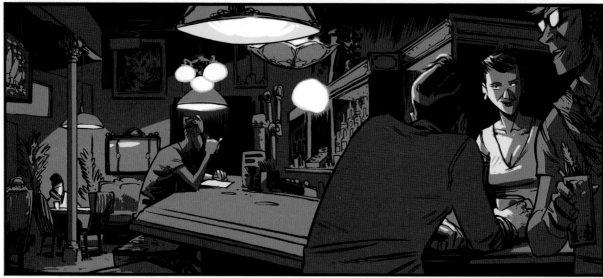

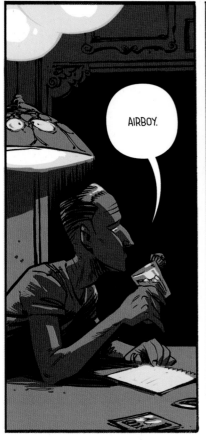

AIRBOY.

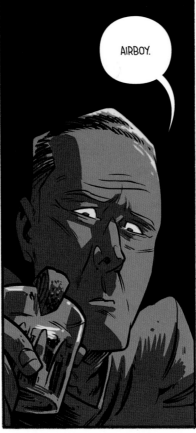

AIRBOY.

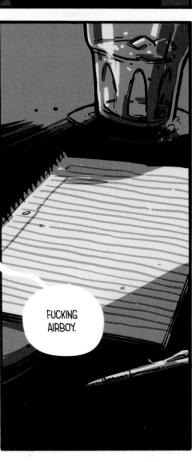

FUCKING AIRBOY.

OPEN

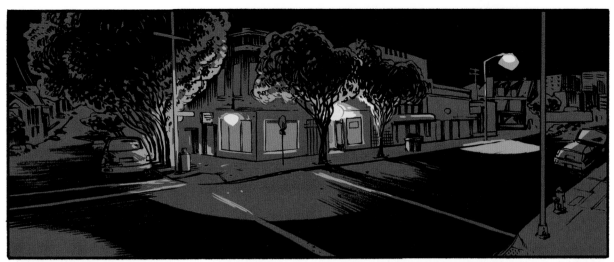

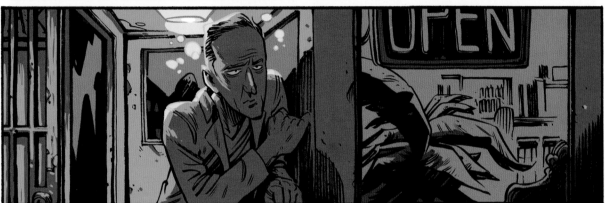

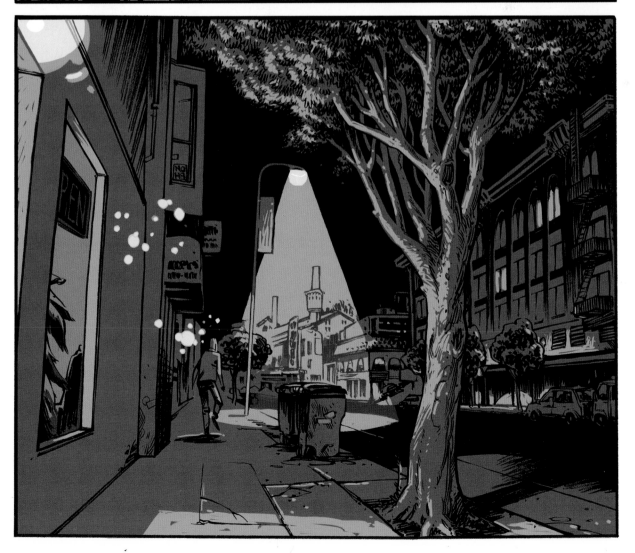

JANN. JAMES' (THEN) WIFE.
YOU CAME IN LATE LAST NIGHT.
TRIED NOT TO WAKE YOU.
WELL YOU COULD HAVE TRIED A LITTLE HARDER, YOU KNOW HOW EARLY I HAVE TO GET UP.
AIRBOY ISN'T COMING. NOT ONE IDEA. AND WE NEED THE MONEY,
I DO ANYWAY.
WHO'S THE ARTIST?
IT'S A BIT EARLY FOR THAT. I JUST SAID, I HAVEN'T A SINGLE THOUGHT IN MY HEAD ABOUT IT.
AND I'M SAYING MAYBE HAVING THE ARTIST FIRST WILL SHAKE SOMETHING UP.

I'M SORRY, JANN.
YOU KEEP SAYING THAT-- HOW "YOU'RE SORRY" --BUT YOU KEEP ON DOING IT.
BACK LATE
WHAT WOULD I DO WITHOUT YOU?
LET'S HOPE YOU NEVER HAVE TO FIND OUT.

GREG HINKLE
I LOVE COMING HERE.
SAN FRANCISCO?
WELL, YOU LIVED HERE FOR HOW LONG BEFORE YOU MOVED TO L.A.? I IMAGINE IT'S LIKE COMING HOME.
SAN FRANCISCO INTERNATIONAL
NO, I MEAN THE AIRPORT-- ANY AIRPORT REALLY, YOU SEE MY DAD WAS--
SO MY IDEAS FOR AIRBOY-- LET ME JUST SAY THAT I HAVE NO IDEAS.
ERR...I GUESS WE'LL TALK ABOUT THAT THEN.
AND THEN I HAD THIS IDEA OF BRINGING AN ARTIST IN FIRST TO SHAKE UP EVERYTHING.
LOTS OF WRITERS AND ARTISTS WORK ON IDEAS TOGETHER.
SURE, BUT ME-- I LIKE TO BE THE ONE WITH THE IDEAS. I'M THE ONE--
NO, THAT'S BULLSHIT, I'M LYING TO MYSELF.
HONESTLY.
IT'S PROBABLY A SIGN OF MY OWN INSECURITIES. I'VE NEVER BEEN TOO SURE IF I'M ANY GOOD AS A WRITER SO IT'S A WAY OF ME KEEPING THE POWER.
SAN FRANCISCO INTERNA

SO WHY ME? WHY'D YOU PICK ME TO WORK WITH?
WELL I TOLD YOU ALREADY, PRETTY MUCH. YOUR ART'S DIFFERENT. I LOVE HOW IT LOOKS AND IT'S FRESH.
IT'S THE KIND OF THING MATT WAGNER WOULD HAVE USED IN *GRENDEL* BACK IN THE DAY.
I FIGURE IF I DO AIRBOY WITH A NORMAL ARTIST, NO ONE'S GOING TO CARE.
FUCK, THEY BARELY READ MY BOOKS AS IT IS UNLESS I'M KILLING BATMAN OR SOME SHIT.
SO INSTEAD WE SHAKE THINGS UP WITH AN ARTISTIC STYLIST.
THAT'S WHAT I AM?
ERR. YEAH. SURE. GO WITH IT.
BELIEVE ME, WHEN YOU GET FURTHER ALONG IN COMICS AND READ THE MESSAGE BOARDS ABOUT YOURSELF, YOU'LL BE CALLED A LOT WORSE.
Mission St
Ninth Street Civic Center
80 Bay Bridge TO 101 NORTH
JCT 80
SO WHERE TO? YOUR PLACE?
JANN DIDN'T WANT US DISRUPTING HER AND SHE DIDN'T WANT TO BOTHER US EITHER...

...SO I GOT US A MOTEL TO WORK OUT OF.
SO LET'S GET STARTED.
GIVE ME SOME DIRECTION. ANYTHING. MAYBE SOME WORDS... YEAH, A LOOSE ASSOCIATION.
AIRBOY.
YEAH, AIRBOY.
LET'S GO GET A DRINK.

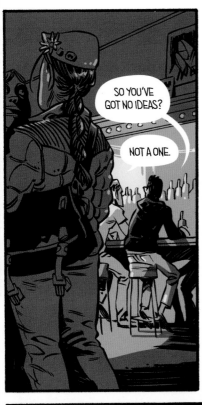

SO YOU'VE GOT NO IDEAS?

NOT A ONE.

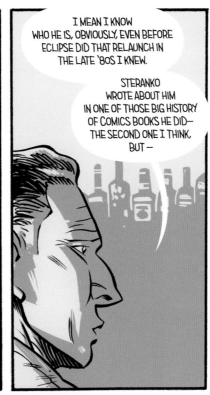

I MEAN I KNOW WHO HE IS, OBVIOUSLY, EVEN BEFORE ECLIPSE DID THAT RELAUNCH IN THE LATE '80S I KNEW.

STERANKO WROTE ABOUT HIM IN ONE OF THOSE BIG HISTORY OF COMICS BOOKS HE DID— THE SECOND ONE I THINK, BUT —

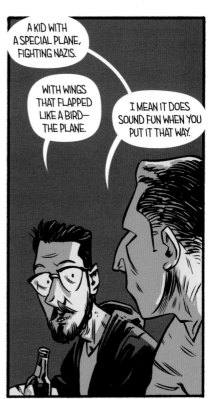

A KID WITH A SPECIAL PLANE, FIGHTING NAZIS.

WITH WINGS THAT FLAPPED LIKE A BIRD— THE PLANE.

I MEAN IT DOES SOUND FUN WHEN YOU PUT IT THAT WAY.

WE COULD DO SOME KIND OF IRONIC TAKE, LAUGH AT IT WHILE WE'RE LAUGHING WITH IT.

NO, I HATE THAT SORT OF THING. HIPSTER WRITERS AND ARTISTS AND THEIR "CLEVER" IRONIC TAKES ON OLD STUFF.

I BLAME DAN CLOWES.

FUCK THE LOT OF THEM.

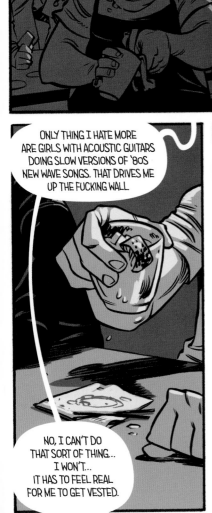

ONLY THING I HATE MORE ARE GIRLS WITH ACOUSTIC GUITARS DOING SLOW VERSIONS OF '80S NEW WAVE SONGS. THAT DRIVES ME UP THE FUCKING WALL

NO, I CAN'T DO THAT SORT OF THING... I WON'T... IT HAS TO FEEL REAL FOR ME TO GET VESTED.

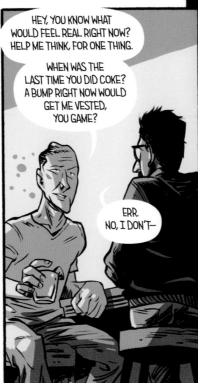

HEY, YOU KNOW WHAT WOULD FEEL REAL RIGHT NOW? HELP ME THINK, FOR ONE THING.

WHEN WAS THE LAST TIME YOU DID COKE? A BUMP RIGHT NOW WOULD GET ME VESTED, YOU GAME?

ERR. NO, I DON'T—

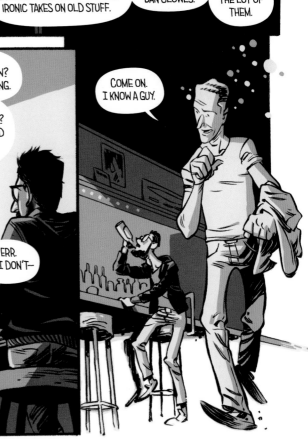

COME ON. I KNOW A GUY.

SO HOW DO YOU KNOW THAT GUY THAT SOLD YOU THIS COKE? HE BASICALLY HAD A WHOLE FUCKING PHARMACY.
IT'S SAN FRANCISCO. YOU MEET PEOPLE.
I LIVED HERE AND I DIDN'T *MEET* PEOPLE. NOT LIKE THAT WEIRDO.
HE'S ACTUALLY QUITE A GIFTED VIOLINIST.
REALLY?
NO.
ENOUGH QUESTIONS. YOU'RE WORSE THAN A NARC. COME ON, IT'S FRIDAY, LET'S PARTY.
BUT I THOUGHT I WAS UP HERE TO WORK. THAT'S THE ONLY REASON MY WIFE SAID IT WAS OKAY.
WE WILL WORK. DON'T WORRY
TOMO
SSSNIFFF
SSNIFF
SNIFFFF
WHERE DID YOU GO?
I DIDN'T LIKE THAT YOU PAID FOR ALL THE DRUGS, SO I GOT US SOME COKE, TOO.
NIIICE. FRESH CHARLIE. WHAT A GENTLEMAN.
SHALL WE AVAIL OURSELVES OF THE BATHROOM?
COME ON, THIS PLACE IS TOO CROWDED.
SSNIFF

I WAS SAYING BEFORE... ABOUT ME, MY DAD, AND AIRPORTS.
WHAT IS IT?
IN A MINUTE. FIRST TRY THIS.
I GOT SOME ECSTASY WHEN I BOUGHT THE BLOW. THE COKE'S SPEEDY, THIS'LL MELLOW YOU OUT.
ERR. FUCK IT, WHAT HAVE I GOT TO LOSE?
SSNIFF
PUNCH. RIGHT IN THE GUT. GO ON. I CAN TAKE IT.
COME ON, THIS PLACE IS DEAD.
OWWY. THAT CHARLIE IS STINGY, BOY.
WELL IT'S MADE ME SOBER AGAIN ALL OF A SUDDEN.
ONLY **ONE** WAY TO CURE THAT...
...TWO MORE!
EVER TRIED HORSE TRANQUILIZER? YOU REALLY SHOULD.
MAYBE IT'S THE NAME. AIRBOY.
MAYBE THAT'S WHAT'S THROWING ME OFF. IT'S SUCH A STUPID FUCKING NAME!
WHOSE FUCKING CAR IS THAT?
GET DOWN OFF IT! FUCK.

CAN I ASK YOU SOMETHING?
SHOOT.
HOW DO YOU HAVE A CAREER AT ALL? ALL THE DRINK AND DRUGS. HOW DO YOU EVEN WRITE?
GOOD QUESTION. TRUTHFULLY, I'M PISSING MY LIFE AWAY. I'M NOT HAPPY AND I DON'T KNOW WHY.
MY CAREER AT DC IS GOING NOWHERE. I'M IN MY DECLINE. I KNOW IT. PEOPLE READING MY BOOKS CAN TELL, FROM THE QUALITY OF MY WORK SLIPPING, I'M SURE.
SO, I DRINK AND DO DRUGS AND PRETEND IT'S GLAMOROUS AND WICKED WHEN IT'S ACTUALLY PATHETIC AND SAD.
YOU ASKED.
THERE. THAT'S THE KIND OF HONESTY YOU ONLY GET FROM DRUGS AND BOOZE.
STILL WANT TO WORK WITH ME?
SURE.
HEY, WE SHOULD SAY HELLO TO HER.
WHY? MAYBE SHE WANTS TO BE BY HERSELF.
WHAT ARE YOU TALKING ABOUT? SHE JUST LOOKED OVER AND SMILED AT US. WELL ME, ANYWAY. OR MAYBE YOU. I DON'T KNOW.
IT'S FRIDAY, NO ONE SHOULD BE STUCK SITTING BY THEMSELVES. COME ON...
"...WE'RE JUST BEING FRIENDLY."
HI.

SHH.

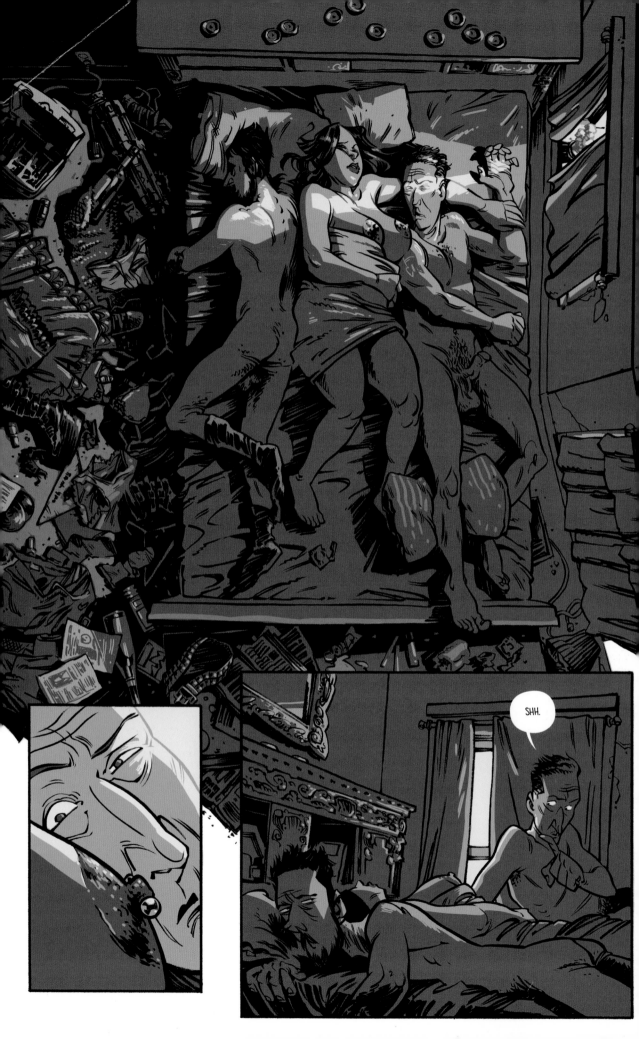

AW, FELL ASLEEP WITH MY CONTACTS IN. HOW DO YOU FEEL?
LIKE SHIT. LIKE THE FLAMING, RANCID SHIT OF LUCIFER HIMSELF.
"FRIENDLY," YOU SAID. "JUST BEING FRIENDLY." JESUS, MY WIFE WILL--
NEVER FIND OUT. NOW QUIET OR YOU'LL WAKE SLEEPING BEAUTY IN THERE.
NEED A PICK-ME-UP. WHERE'S THAT CHARLIE YOU GOT?
THE COKE? HERE.
WHY DO YOU KEEP CALLING IT CHARLIE, ANYWAY?
I THINK IT'S BRITISH SLANG, NAMED FOR CHARLIE COKER, THE CHARACTER MICHAEL CAINE PLAYS IN *THE ITALIAN JOB*.
I COULD BE WRONG, BUT IT'S WHAT I LIKE TO BELIEVE ANYWAY--
YIKES!

IN THE NAME OF ALL THAT'S HOLY, PUT SOME PANTS ON.
THAT ANACONDA OF YOURS IS UNSETTLING TO SEE ON A *GOOD* DAY AND THIS IS NOT A GOOD DAY.
SORRY.
HERE.
NICE, NOW GO PUT ON THOSE BOXERS AND I'LL CHOP OUT A FEW--
HEY, WHERE DID YOU GET THIS?
WHAT GUY?
THAT GUY. AT THE LAST BAR.
YOUR FRIEND WITH THE WAXED MUSTACHE.
HE WASN'T MY FRIEND, I'D JUST MET HIM. I DON'T EVEN REMEMBER HIS NAME.
DONALD. NO, DAN... DANNY.
SEE, YOU KNOW MORE THAN ME ABOUT THE GUY. I'LL TELL YOU WHAT I DO KNOW...
...IN THE TIME SINCE THEN AND NOW, THE "CHARLIE'S" TURNED FROM WHITE TO GOLDEN BROWN.
WHICH MEANS?

I'M PRETTY SURE WE WERE SNORTING HEROIN LAST NIGHT, WHICH IS A FIRST EVEN FOR ME.
HEROIN.
HEROIN!
HOW DID *THAT* HAPPEN?
DON'T ASK ME, *LOU REED*, YOU'RE THE ONE WHO BOUGHT IT.
PLUS THE X AND THE COKE THAT *WAS* COKE-- YOURS-- IT'S A WONDER WE DIDN'T DIE.
RELAX. PEOPLE HAVE DONE A LOT WORSE.
WHO, HUNTER S. THOMPSON? FUCK.
HERE, I STILL HAVE SOME OF MINE. WHITE AS MY SOUL.
LET'S CHOP IT UP AND THEN HOPEFULLY EVERYTHING WILL MAKE SENSE.
OH, I DOUBT IT.
GENTLEMEN...

...THIS BEHAVIOR WILL NOT STAND!

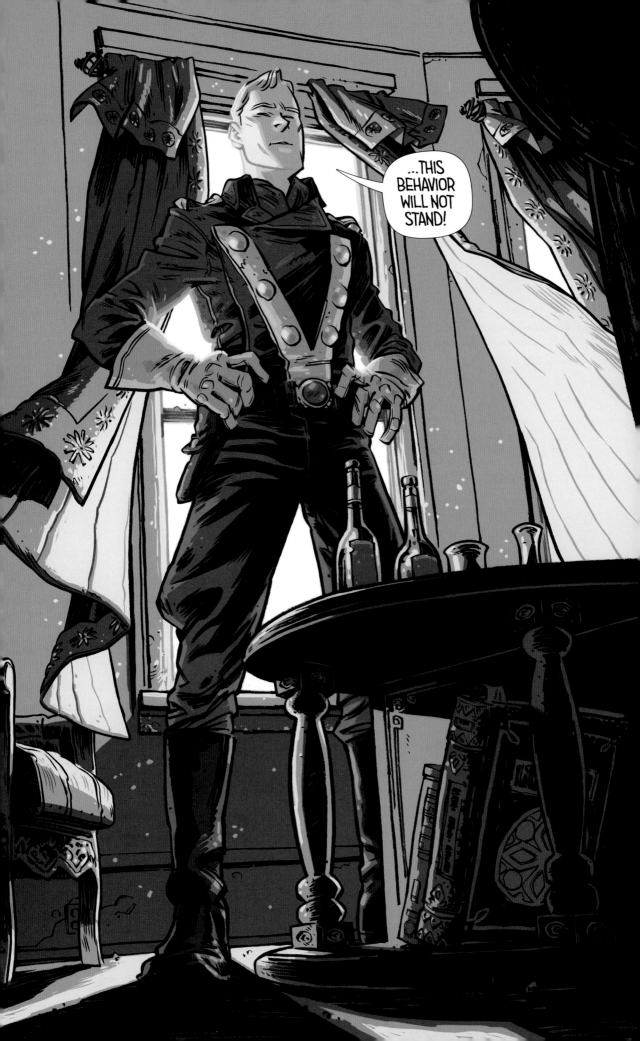

CHAPTER 2

AIRBOY

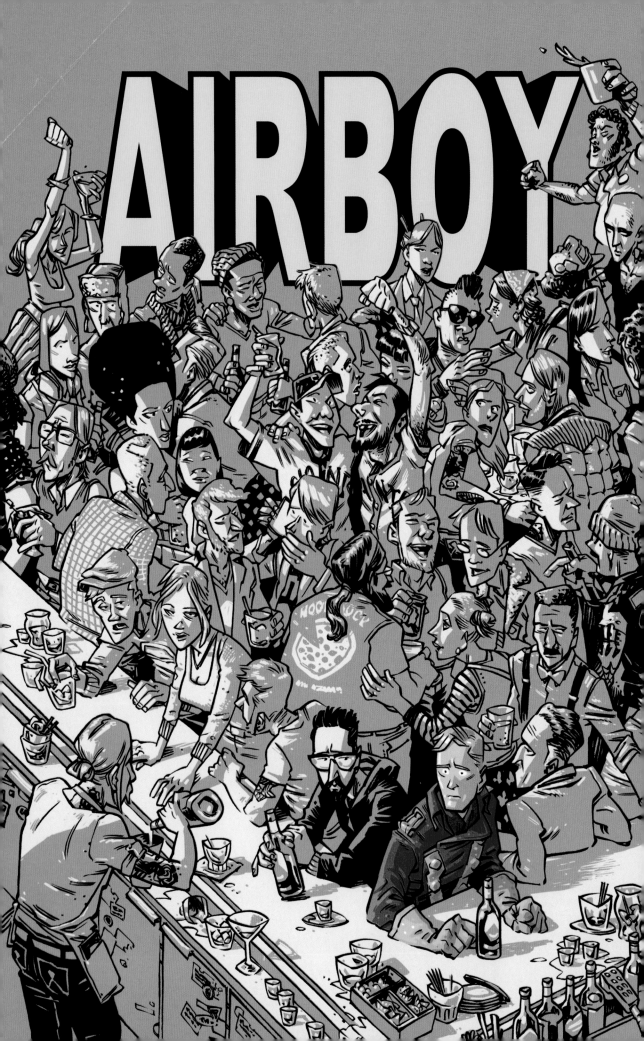

RUN!
RUN!
I'M RUNNING!
I'M RUNNING!

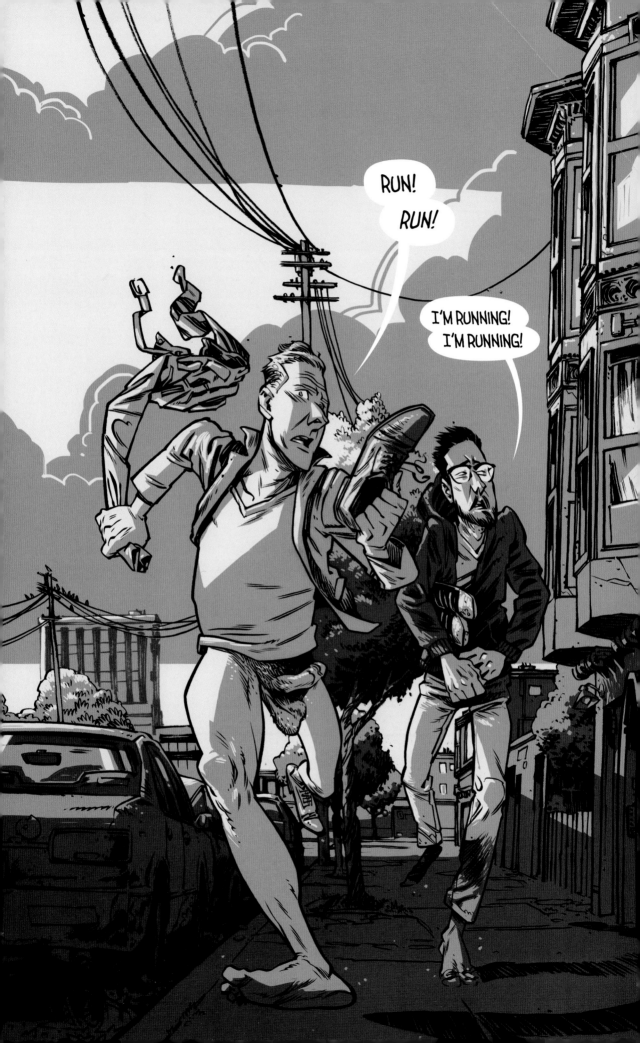

HERE! GET IN HERE!
YEAH.
AERRRRR
HUFF HUFF
HEY, WHY WERE YOU RUNNING?
WHY WERE YOU?
I ASKED FIRST.
ME TOO! I HAD ONE TOO.
I HAD A HALLUCINATION AND IT FREAKED ME THE FUCK OUT.
WELL THAT'S GOING TO BE EXPECTED WITH THE DRUG COCKTAIL THAT'S RUNNING THROUGH US.

GOD, LOOK AT ME, MY DICK'S OUT.
I LOST A FUCKING SOCK.
SO WHAT DID YOU SEE?
WELL, I GUESS IT'S TO BE EXPECTED WITH WHAT WE'RE WORKING ON--
TRYING TO GET THE IDEA TO WORK ON, ANYWAY--
BUT I SAW AIRBOY, STANDING THERE, CALM AND BRIGHT AS DAY.
THAT'S NUTS, I SAW EXACTLY THE SAME THING. CRAZY NUTS.
AIRBOY. RED SHIRT. BOOTS. *AIRBOY.*
PEOPLE HAVE THE SAME VISIONS ALL THE TIME.
HAVE *YOU* EVER? SEEN THE SAME THING WHEN YOU WERE FUCKED UP AS SOMEONE WITH YOU?
NO.
ME NEITHER.
WELL, I GUESS WITH ALL OF THE DRUGS IN US, LIKE I SAID--
I DON'T KNOW WHY YOU RAN OFF...

...BUT WILL YOU HELP ME?
I'M TRYING TO WORK OUT WHERE I AM.
HERE, TAKE MY HAND--
NO, WAIT... **SHAKE** MY HAND, THAT'S WHAT I MEANT.

I'M JAMES ROBINSON.
I'M DAVID NELSON, BUT FOLKS CALL ME **AIRBOY**.
ERR, HELLO.
OVER HERE.
I'M GREG HINKLE.

BALANCOIRE
DOC'S CLOCK
COCKTAIL TIME

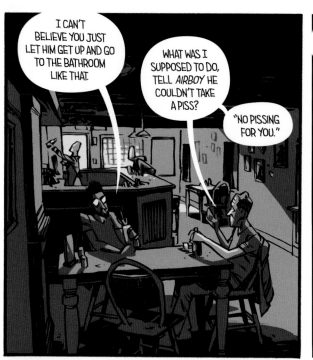

I CAN'T BELIEVE YOU JUST LET HIM GET UP AND GO TO THE BATHROOM LIKE THAT.

WHAT WAS I SUPPOSED TO DO, TELL *AIRBOY* HE COULDN'T TAKE A PISS?

"NO PISSING FOR YOU."

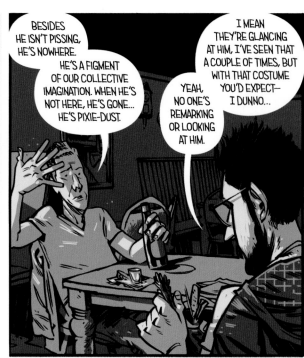

BESIDES HE ISN'T PISSING, HE'S NOWHERE. HE'S A FIGMENT OF OUR COLLECTIVE IMAGINATION. WHEN HE'S NOT HERE, HE'S GONE... HE'S PIXIE-DUST.

YEAH, NO ONE'S REMARKING OR LOOKING AT HIM.

I MEAN THEY'RE GLANCING AT HIM, I'VE SEEN THAT A COUPLE OF TIMES, BUT WITH THAT COSTUME YOU'D EXPECT— I DUNNO...

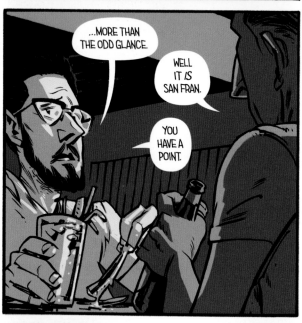

...MORE THAN THE ODD GLANCE.

WELL IT *IS* SAN FRAN.

YOU HAVE A POINT.

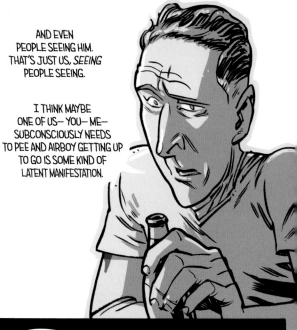

AND EVEN PEOPLE SEEING HIM. THAT'S JUST US, *SEEING* PEOPLE SEEING.

I THINK MAYBE ONE OF US— YOU— ME— SUBCONSCIOUSLY NEEDS TO PEE AND AIRBOY GETTING UP TO GO IS SOME KIND OF LATENT MANIFESTATION.

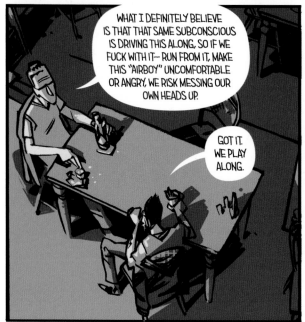

WHAT I DEFINITELY BELIEVE IS THAT THAT SAME SUBCONSCIOUS IS DRIVING THIS ALONG, SO IF WE FUCK WITH IT— RUN FROM IT, MAKE THIS "AIRBOY" UNCOMFORTABLE OR ANGRY, WE RISK MESSING OUR OWN HEADS UP.

GOT IT. WE PLAY ALONG.

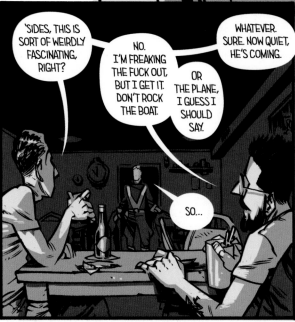

'SIDES, THIS IS SORT OF WEIRDLY FASCINATING, RIGHT?

NO. I'M FREAKING THE FUCK OUT, BUT I GET IT. DON'T ROCK THE BOAT.

OR THE PLANE, I GUESS I SHOULD SAY.

WHATEVER. SURE. NOW QUIET, HE'S COMING.

SO...

...I DON'T WANT TO SEEM RUDE, GUYS. I DON'T WANT TO OFFEND YOU...
...BUT ARE YOU SUPER-VILLAINS?
DO WE LOOK LIKE SUPER-VILLAINS? HERE, SIT.
WELL, NO. YOU DON'T. MAYBE THE *STOOGES* OF A SUPER-VILLAIN THOUGH.
YOU STILL TRYING NOT TO BE RUDE?
GREG. *SSHHH.*
OH RIGHT, *SORRY.* I SHOULD BE MORE CAREFUL WHAT I SAY, IRON ACE IS ALWAYS GETTING ONTO ME ABOUT THAT.
IRON ACE?
I'LL TELL YOU LATER.
NO, WE'RE NOT VILLAINS OR-- ERR-- STOOGES, WHY D'YOU ASK?
I FEEL LIKE A VILLAIN HAS MESSED WITH MY HEAD AND I'M IN SOME KIND OF EVIL DREAM.
THIS ISN'T EARTH-- NOT *MY* EARTH ANYWAY. THIS ONE'S-- WELL-- IT'S SO *UGLY.* THE PEOPLE-- WHY DOES EVERYONE SEEM LIKE THEY HAVE NO CLOTHES?
WHAT DO YOU MEAN? EVERYONE'S DRESSED.

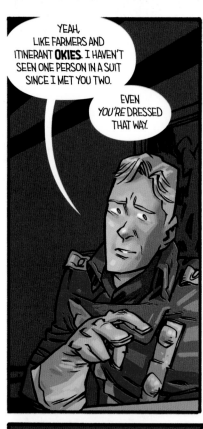

YEAH, LIKE FARMERS AND ITINERANT **OKIES**. I HAVEN'T SEEN ONE PERSON IN A SUIT SINCE I MET YOU TWO.

EVEN *YOU'RE* DRESSED THAT WAY.

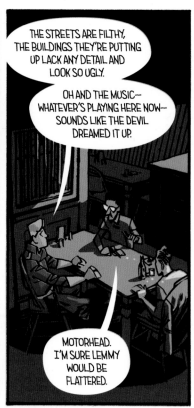

THE STREETS ARE FILTHY, THE BUILDINGS THEY'RE PUTTING UP LACK ANY DETAIL AND LOOK SO UGLY.

OH AND THE MUSIC— WHATEVER'S PLAYING HERE NOW— SOUNDS LIKE THE DEVIL DREAMED IT UP.

MOTORHEAD. I'M SURE LEMMY WOULD BE FLATTERED.

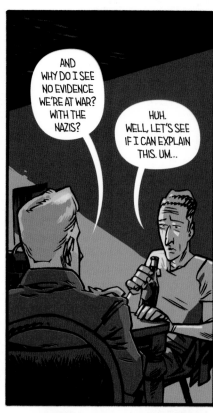

AND WHY DO I SEE NO EVIDENCE WE'RE AT WAR? WITH THE NAZIS?

HUH. WELL, LET'S SEE IF I CAN EXPLAIN THIS. UM...

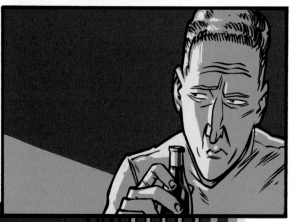

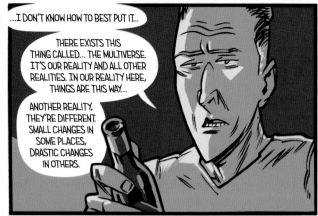

...I DON'T KNOW HOW TO BEST PUT IT...

THERE EXISTS THIS THING CALLED... THE MULTIVERSE. IT'S OUR REALITY AND ALL OTHER REALITIES. IN OUR REALITY HERE, THINGS ARE THIS WAY...

ANOTHER REALITY, THEY'RE DIFFERENT. SMALL CHANGES IN SOME PLACES, DRASTIC CHANGES IN OTHERS.

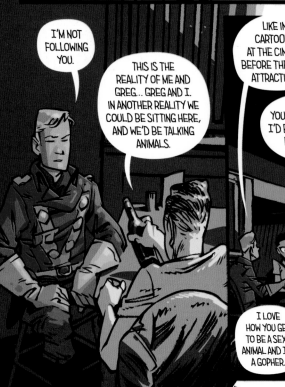

I'M NOT FOLLOWING YOU.

THIS IS THE REALITY OF ME AND GREG... GREG AND I. IN ANOTHER REALITY WE COULD BE SITTING HERE, AND WE'D BE TALKING ANIMALS.

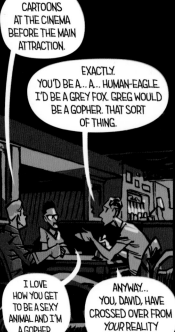

LIKE IN CARTOONS AT THE CINEMA BEFORE THE MAIN ATTRACTION.

EXACTLY. YOU'D BE A... A... HUMAN-EAGLE. I'D BE A GREY FOX. GREG WOULD BE A GOPHER. THAT SORT OF THING.

I LOVE HOW YOU GET TO BE A SEXY ANIMAL AND I'M A GOPHER.

ANYWAY... YOU, DAVID, HAVE CROSSED OVER FROM *YOUR* REALITY TO *OURS*.

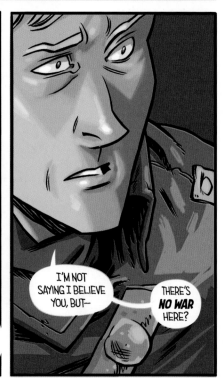

I'M NOT SAYING I BELIEVE YOU, BUT—

THERE'S **NO WAR** HERE?

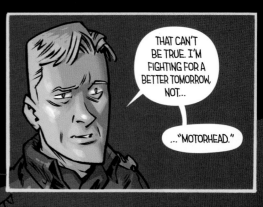

THAT CAN'T BE TRUE. I'M FIGHTING FOR A BETTER TOMORROW, NOT...

..."MOTORHEAD."

OH, THERE WAS, BUT IT'S OVER.

AND THE NAZIS *WON*? THAT'S TERRIBLE.

STILL, IT WOULD EXPLAIN ALL THE *FILTH* AND *HORROR* ON THE STREETS.

HORROR? GOD, IT'S NOT *THAT* BAD, IS IT? AND NO, WE WON. THE ALLIES.

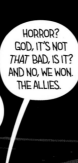

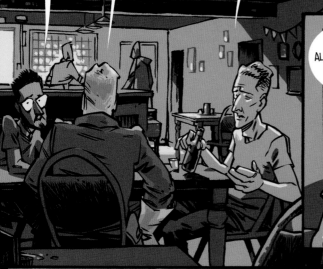

WHY ARE YOU TELLING HIM ALL THIS? I THOUGHT YOU WANTED HIM HAPPY AND CALM.

IT SEEMED THE RIGHT THING. TALK TO HIM LIKE WE'RE ALL IN A COMIC TOGETHER.

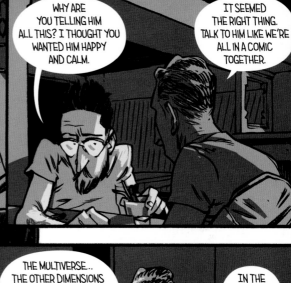

HOW DO YOU KNOW ALL THIS ANYWAY?

I HEARD WHAT YOU SAID, JUST THEN, BY THE WAY. WHY WOULD YOU WANT IT TO SEEM LIKE WE'RE ALL IN A COMIC?

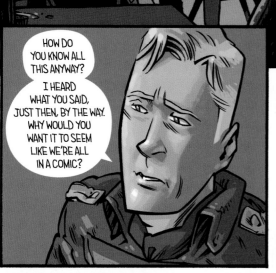

THE MULTIVERSE... THE OTHER DIMENSIONS AND EVERYTHING I TOLD YOU. IT'S A FICTION IN COMIC BOOKS. DC COMICS AND MARVEL COMICS BOTH.

IN THE WORLD OF COMIC BOOK CHARACTERS.

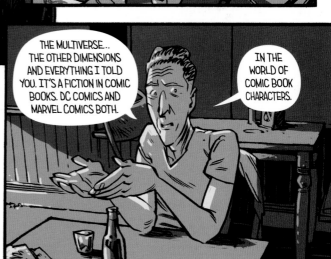

AND... AND... UM...ERR...

...THAT'S WHAT **YOU** ARE, DAVID.

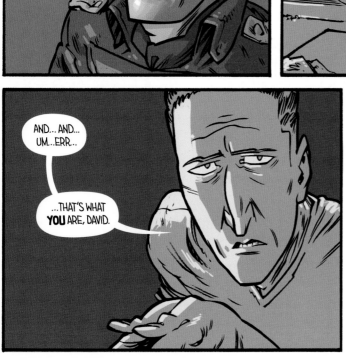

YOU'RE A *CHARACTER* IN A COMIC BOOK.

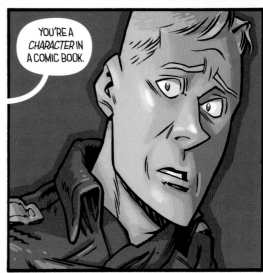

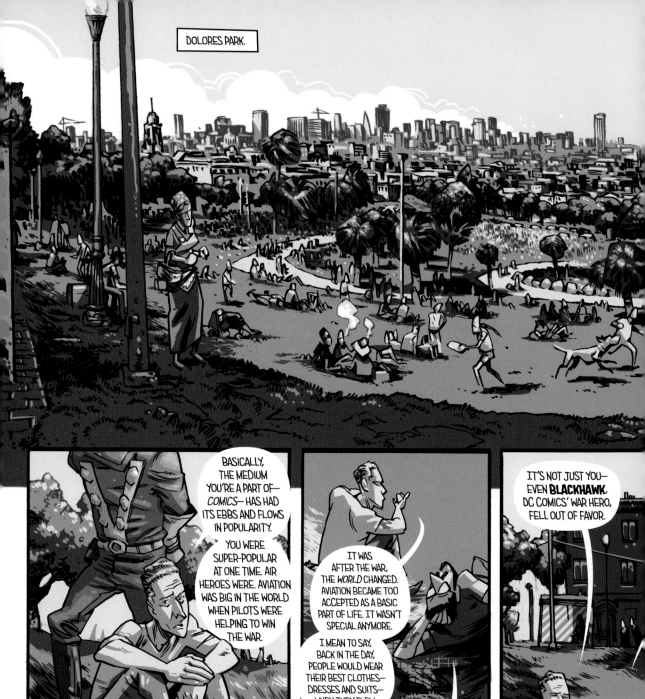

DOLORES PARK.

BASICALLY, THE MEDIUM YOU'RE A PART OF— COMICS— HAS HAD ITS EBBS AND FLOWS IN POPULARITY.

YOU WERE SUPER-POPULAR AT ONE TIME. AIR HEROES WERE. AVIATION WAS BIG IN THE WORLD WHEN PILOTS WERE HELPING TO WIN THE WAR.

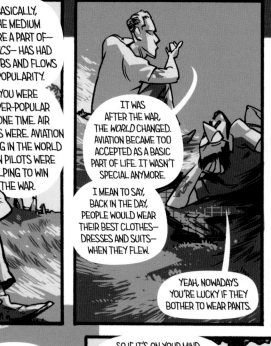

IT WAS AFTER THE WAR, THE WORLD CHANGED. AVIATION BECAME TOO ACCEPTED AS A BASIC PART OF LIFE. IT WASN'T SPECIAL ANYMORE.

I MEAN TO SAY, BACK IN THE DAY, PEOPLE WOULD WEAR THEIR BEST CLOTHES— DRESSES AND SUITS— WHEN THEY FLEW.

YEAH, NOWADAYS YOU'RE LUCKY IF THEY BOTHER TO WEAR PANTS.

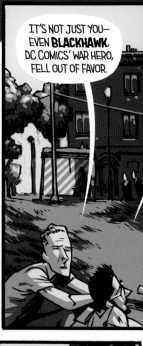

IT'S NOT JUST YOU— EVEN **BLACKHAWK**, DC COMICS' WAR HERO, FELL OUT OF FAVOR.

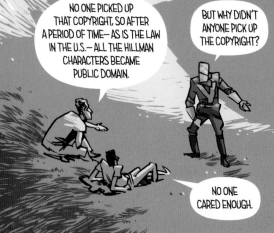

NO ONE PICKED UP THAT COPYRIGHT, SO AFTER A PERIOD OF TIME— AS IS THE LAW IN THE U.S.— ALL THE HILLMAN CHARACTERS BECAME PUBLIC DOMAIN.

BUT WHY DIDN'T ANYONE PICK UP THE COPYRIGHT?

NO ONE CARED ENOUGH.

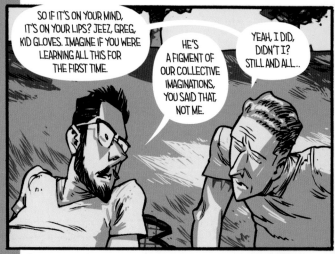

SO IF IT'S ON YOUR MIND, IT'S ON YOUR LIPS? JEEZ, GREG, KID GLOVES. IMAGINE IF YOU WERE LEARNING ALL THIS FOR THE FIRST TIME.

HE'S A FIGMENT OF OUR COLLECTIVE IMAGINATIONS, YOU SAID THAT, NOT ME.

YEAH, I DID, DIDN'T I? STILL AND ALL...

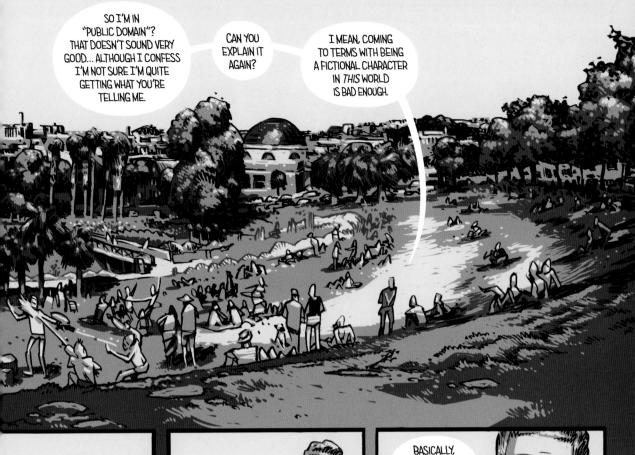

SO I'M IN "PUBLIC DOMAIN"? THAT DOESN'T SOUND VERY GOOD... ALTHOUGH I CONFESS I'M NOT SURE I'M QUITE GETTING WHAT YOU'RE TELLING ME.

CAN YOU EXPLAIN IT AGAIN?

I MEAN, COMING TO TERMS WITH BEING A FICTIONAL CHARACTER IN *THIS* WORLD IS BAD ENOUGH.

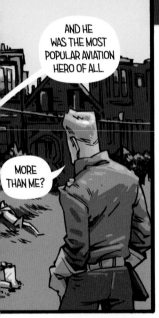

AND HE WAS THE MOST POPULAR AVIATION HERO OF ALL

MORE THAN ME?

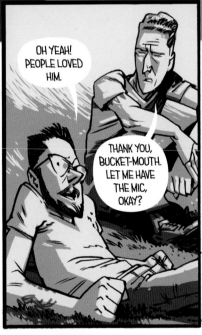

OH YEAH! PEOPLE LOVED HIM.

THANK YOU, BUCKET-MOUTH. LET ME HAVE THE MIC, OKAY?

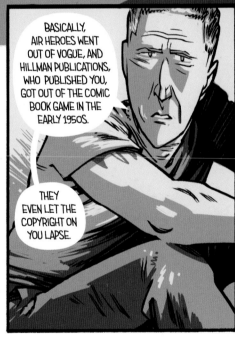

BASICALLY, AIR HEROES WENT OUT OF VOGUE, AND HILLMAN PUBLICATIONS, WHO PUBLISHED YOU, GOT OUT OF THE COMIC BOOK GAME IN THE EARLY 1950S.

THEY EVEN LET THE COPYRIGHT ON YOU LAPSE.

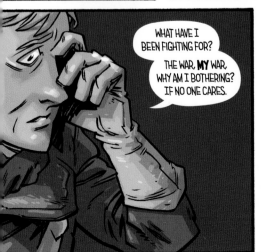

WHAT HAVE I BEEN FIGHTING FOR? THE WAR, **MY** WAR, WHY AM I BOTHERING? IF NO ONE CARES.

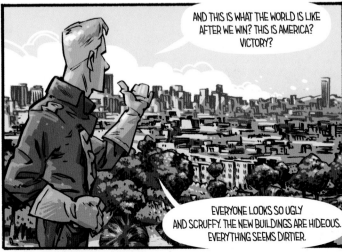

AND THIS IS WHAT THE WORLD IS LIKE AFTER WE WIN? THIS IS AMERICA? VICTORY?

EVERYONE LOOKS SO UGLY AND SCRUFFY. THE NEW BUILDINGS ARE HIDEOUS. EVERYTHING SEEMS DIRTIER.

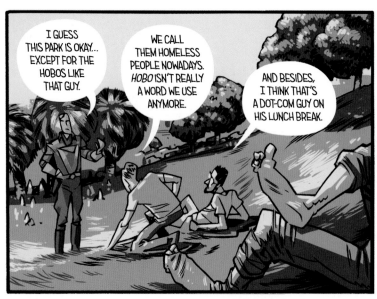

I GUESS THIS PARK IS OKAY... EXCEPT FOR THE HOBOS LIKE THAT GUY.

WE CALL THEM HOMELESS PEOPLE NOWADAYS. *HOBO* ISN'T REALLY A WORD WE USE ANYMORE.

AND BESIDES, I THINK THAT'S A DOT-COM GUY ON HIS LUNCH BREAK.

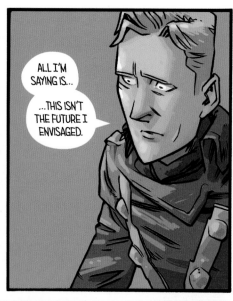

ALL I'M SAYING IS...

...THIS ISN'T THE FUTURE I ENVISAGED.

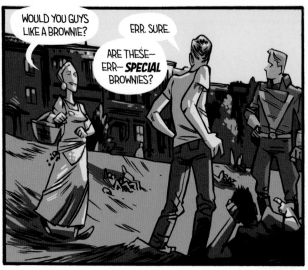

WOULD YOU GUYS LIKE A BROWNIE?

ERR. SURE.

ARE THESE— ERR— *SPECIAL* BROWNIES?

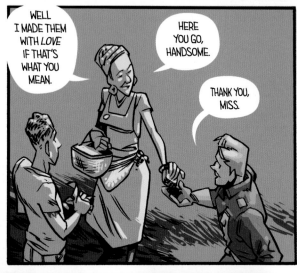

WELL I MADE THEM WITH *LOVE* IF THAT'S WHAT YOU MEAN.

HERE YOU GO, HANDSOME.

THANK YOU, MISS.

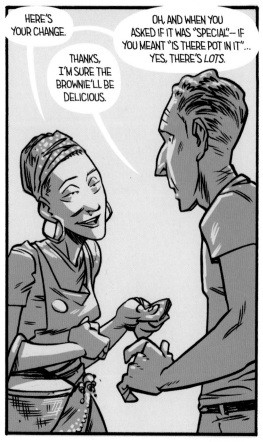

HERE'S YOUR CHANGE.

OH, AND WHEN YOU ASKED IF IT WAS "SPECIAL"— IF YOU MEANT "IS THERE POT IN IT"... YES, THERE'S *LOTS*.

THANKS, I'M SURE THE BROWNIE'LL BE DELICIOUS.

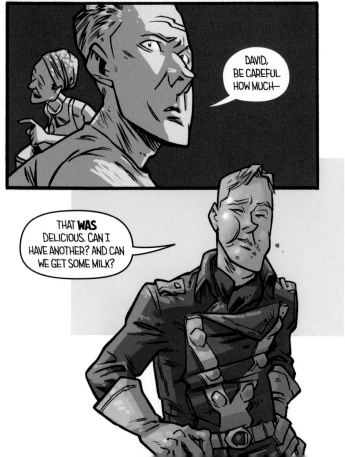

DAVID, BE CAREFUL HOW MUCH—

THAT **WAS** DELICIOUS. CAN I HAVE ANOTHER? AND CAN WE GET SOME MILK?

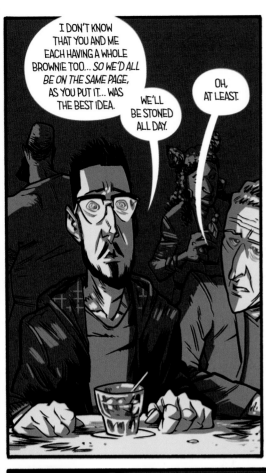

I DON'T KNOW THAT YOU AND ME EACH HAVING A WHOLE BROWNIE TOO... *SO WE'D ALL BE ON THE SAME PAGE*, AS YOU PUT IT... WAS THE BEST IDEA.

WE'LL BE STONED ALL DAY.

OH, AT LEAST.

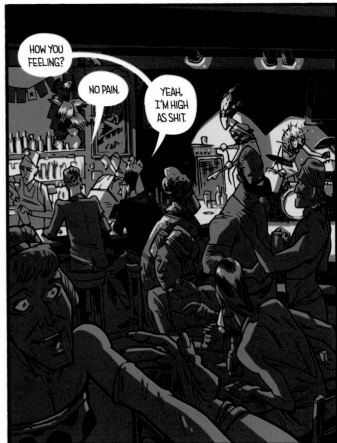

HOW YOU FEELING?

NO PAIN.

YEAH, I'M HIGH AS SHIT.

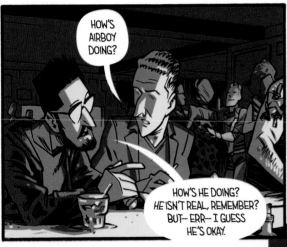

HOW'S AIRBOY DOING?

HOW'S HE DOING? *HE* ISN'T REAL, REMEMBER? BUT-- ERR-- I GUESS HE'S OKAY.

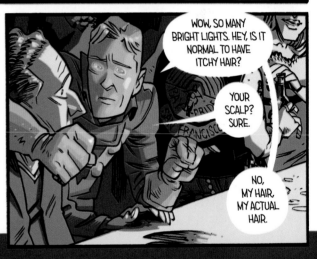

WOW, SO MANY BRIGHT LIGHTS. HEY, IS IT NORMAL TO HAVE ITCHY HAIR?

YOUR SCALP? SURE.

NO, MY HAIR, MY ACTUAL HAIR.

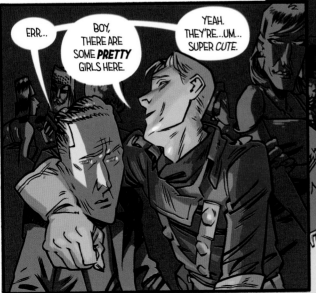

ERR...

BOY, THERE ARE SOME *PRETTY* GIRLS HERE.

YEAH. THEY'RE... UM... SUPER *CUTE*.

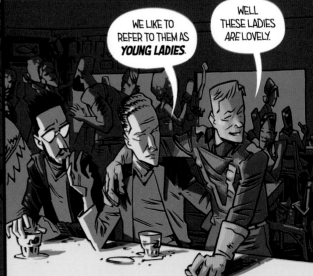

WE LIKE TO REFER TO THEM AS *YOUNG LADIES*.

WELL THESE LADIES *ARE* LOVELY.

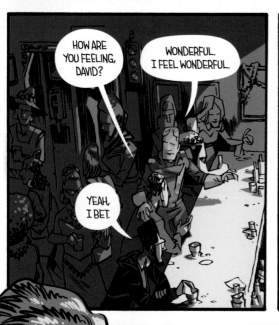

HOW ARE YOU FEELING, DAVID?

WONDERFUL. I FEEL WONDERFUL.

YEAH, I BET.

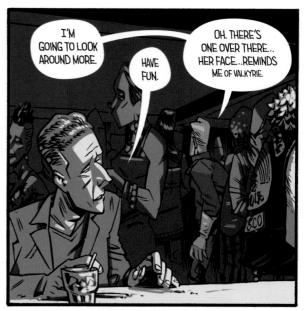

I'M GOING TO LOOK AROUND MORE.

HAVE FUN.

OH. THERE'S ONE OVER THERE... HER FACE...REMINDS ME OF VALKYRIE.

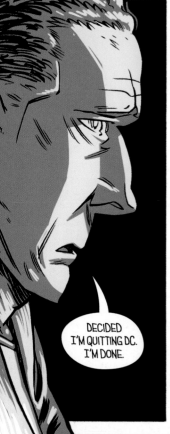

DECIDED I'M QUITTING DC. I'M DONE.

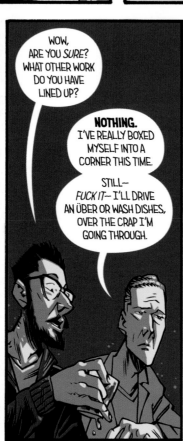

WOW, ARE YOU *SURE?* WHAT OTHER WORK DO YOU HAVE LINED UP?

NOTHING. I'VE REALLY BOXED MYSELF INTO A CORNER THIS TIME.

STILL— *FUCK IT*— I'LL DRIVE AN ÜBER OR WASH DISHES, OVER THE CRAP I'M GOING THROUGH.

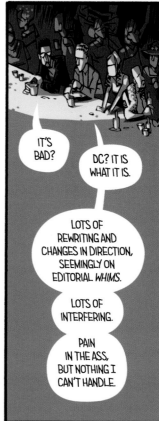

IT'S BAD?

DC? IT IS WHAT IT IS.

LOTS OF REWRITING AND CHANGES IN DIRECTION, SEEMINGLY ON EDITORIAL *WHIMS.*

LOTS OF INTERFERING.

PAIN IN THE ASS, BUT NOTHING I CAN'T HANDLE.

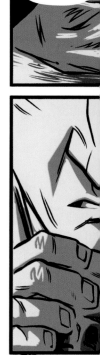

AND THEY PAY PRETTY GOOD.

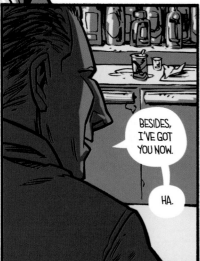

BESIDES, I'VE GOT YOU NOW.

HA.

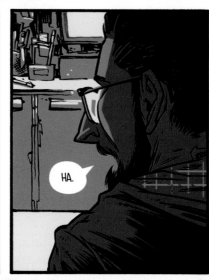

HA.

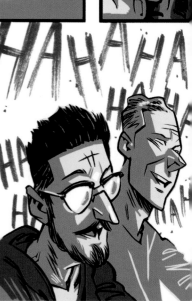

HAHAHA
HA
HA
HA

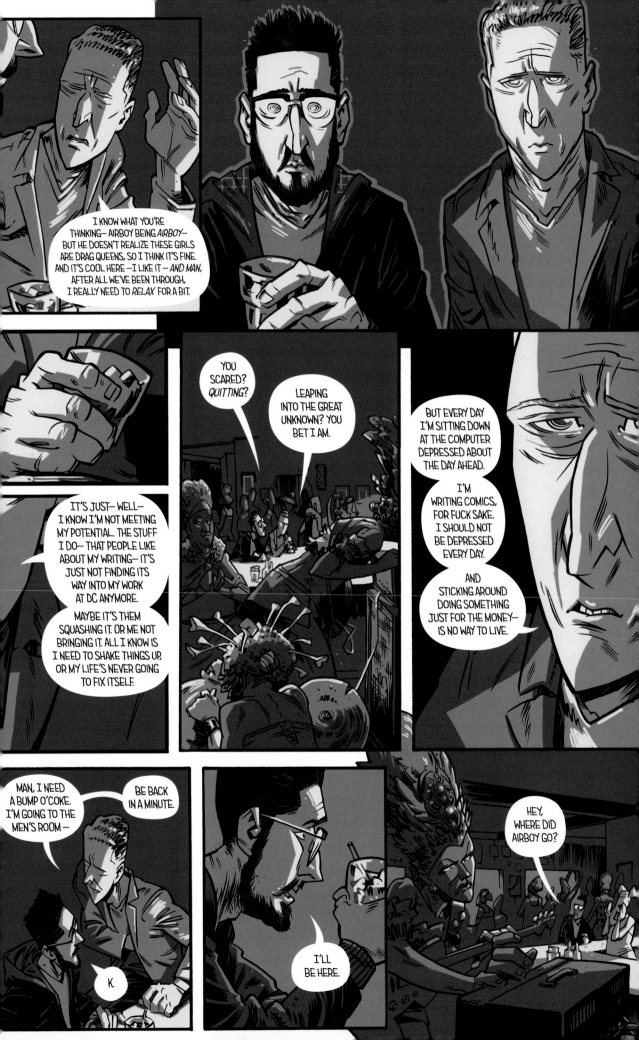

I KNOW WHAT YOU'RE THINKING— AIRBOY BEING *AIRBOY*— BUT HE DOESN'T REALIZE THESE GIRLS ARE DRAG QUEENS, SO I THINK IT'S FINE. AND IT'S COOL HERE —I LIKE IT — *AND MAN*, AFTER ALL WE'VE BEEN THROUGH, I REALLY NEED TO *RELAX* FOR A BIT.

YOU SCARED? *QUITTING?*

LEAPING INTO THE GREAT UNKNOWN? YOU BET I AM.

BUT EVERY DAY I'M SITTING DOWN AT THE COMPUTER DEPRESSED ABOUT THE DAY AHEAD.

I'M WRITING COMICS, FOR FUCK SAKE. I SHOULD NOT BE DEPRESSED EVERY DAY.

AND STICKING AROUND DOING SOMETHING JUST FOR THE MONEY— IS NO WAY TO LIVE.

IT'S JUST— WELL— I KNOW I'M NOT MEETING MY POTENTIAL. THE STUFF I DO— THAT PEOPLE LIKE ABOUT MY WRITING— IT'S JUST NOT FINDING ITS WAY INTO MY WORK AT DC ANYMORE.

MAYBE IT'S THEM SQUASHING IT. OR ME NOT BRINGING IT. ALL I KNOW IS I NEED TO SHAKE THINGS UP, OR MY LIFE'S NEVER GOING TO FIX ITSELF.

MAN, I NEED A BUMP O' COKE. I'M GOING TO THE MEN'S ROOM —

BE BACK IN A MINUTE.

HEY, WHERE DID AIRBOY GO?

K.

I'LL BE HERE.

AHHH.
THAT'S GREAT.
GREAT.
NO, NO, TOO MUCH TEETH.
THAT'S BETTER, *THAT'S* GOOD.
AHH.

OH.
THANK YOU, MISS.
THANK YOU.
THANK YOU.
AIRBOY?...
...IS THAT YOU?

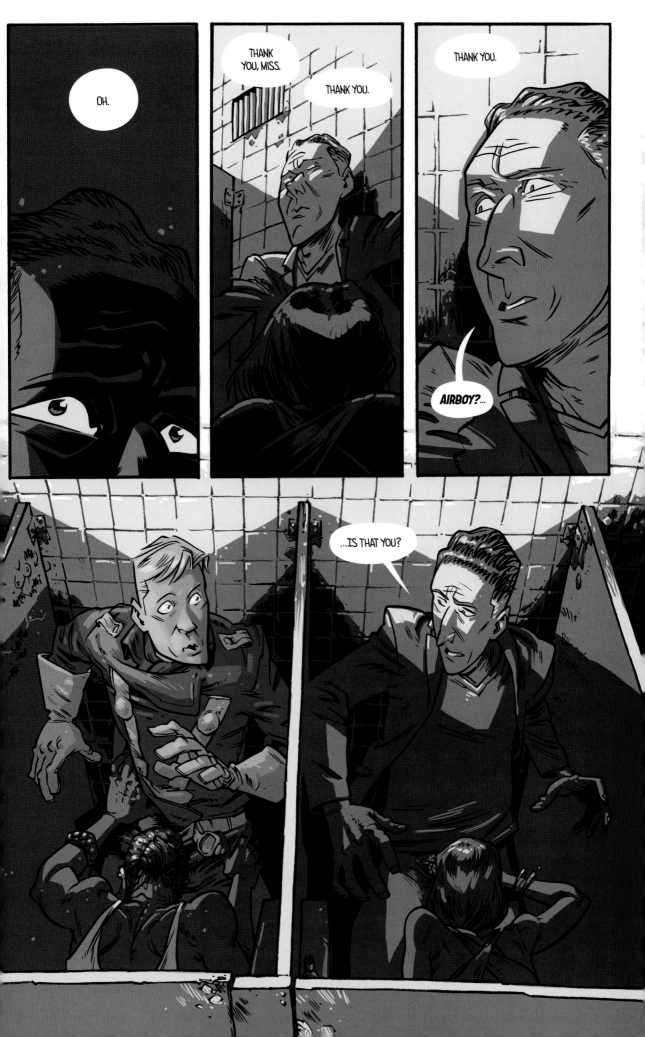

YEAH, IN THE CUBICLE NEXT TO MINE.
WILD, RIGHT?
IN YOUR HEAD.
WHAT?
AIRBOY'S *NOT REAL*. HOW MANY TIMES DO I HAVE TO REMIND YOU? HE'S IN OUR HEADS.
YOU GOT BLOWN IN A STALL. JUST YOU. HE WASN'T THERE.
BLOWN IN A STALL.
YOU MAKE IT SOUND SO *CHEAP*.
WHAT? THERE WAS A DEEP MEETING OF THE MINDS?
SHE WAS VERY SWEET.
ANYWAY, *QUIET*, HERE COMES THE GREAT LOVER.
YOU... **YOU...**
...YOU BASTARDS!

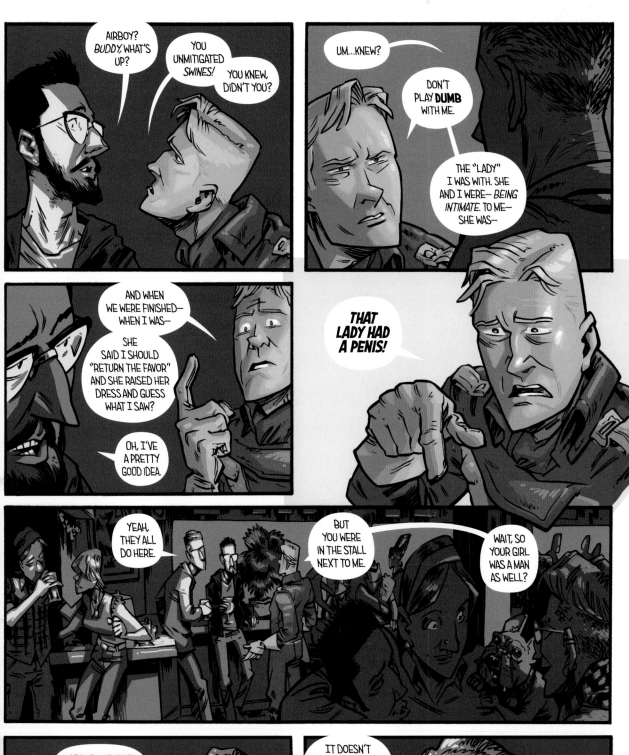

Panel 1:
AIRBOY? *BUDDY,* WHAT'S UP?

YOU UNMITIGATED *SWINES!* YOU KNEW, DIDN'T YOU?

Panel 2:
UM...KNEW?

DON'T PLAY **DUMB** WITH ME.

THE "LADY" I WAS WITH. SHE AND I WERE— *BEING INTIMATE.* TO ME— SHE WAS—

Panel 3:
AND WHEN WE WERE FINISHED— WHEN I WAS—

SHE SAID I SHOULD "RETURN THE FAVOR" AND SHE RAISED HER DRESS AND GUESS WHAT I SAW?

OH, I'VE A PRETTY GOOD IDEA.

THAT LADY HAD A PENIS!

Panel 4:
YEAH, THEY ALL DO HERE.

BUT YOU WERE IN THE STALL NEXT TO ME.

WAIT, SO YOUR GIRL WAS A MAN AS WELL?

Panel 5:
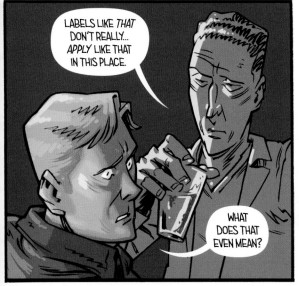
LABELS LIKE *THAT* DON'T REALLY... *APPLY* LIKE THAT IN THIS PLACE.

WHAT DOES THAT EVEN MEAN?

Panel 6:
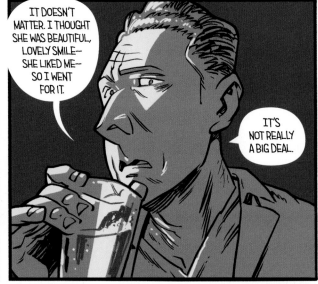
IT DOESN'T MATTER. I THOUGHT SHE WAS BEAUTIFUL, LOVELY SMILE— SHE LIKED ME— SO I WENT FOR IT.

IT'S NOT REALLY A BIG DEAL.

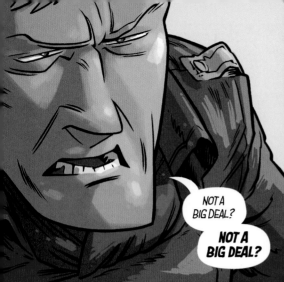

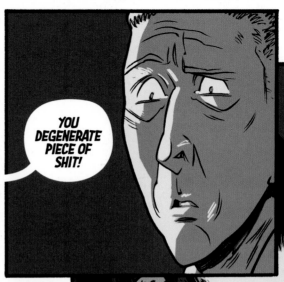

NOT A BIG DEAL?

NOT A BIG DEAL?

YOU DEGENERATE PIECE OF SHIT!

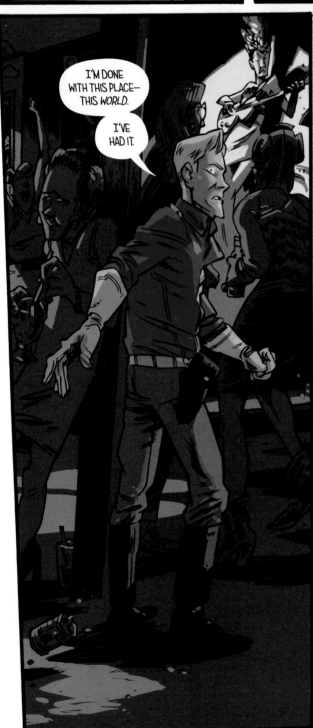

I'M DONE WITH THIS PLACE— THIS *WORLD*.

I'VE HAD IT.

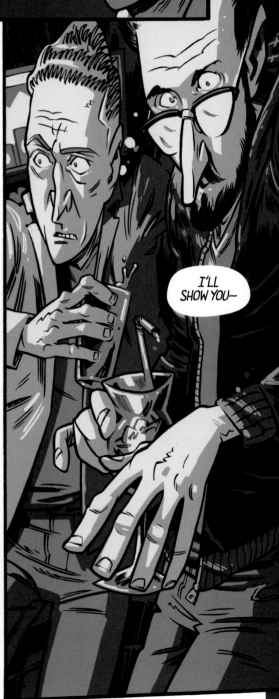

I'LL SHOW YOU—

I'LL SHOW YOU WHAT A REAL DAY LOOKS LIKE!
WELCOME TO MY WORLD-- ONE OF DANGER, SURE, BUT A PLACE OF HONOR AND HEROISM TOO.
OHHH BOY.
HERE, EVERYTHING YOUR PATHETIC, SORRY LIVES ARE LACKING..

...NOW TAKE A GOOD LOOK!
DID YOU SPIKE MY DRINK?
UM. MAYBE.

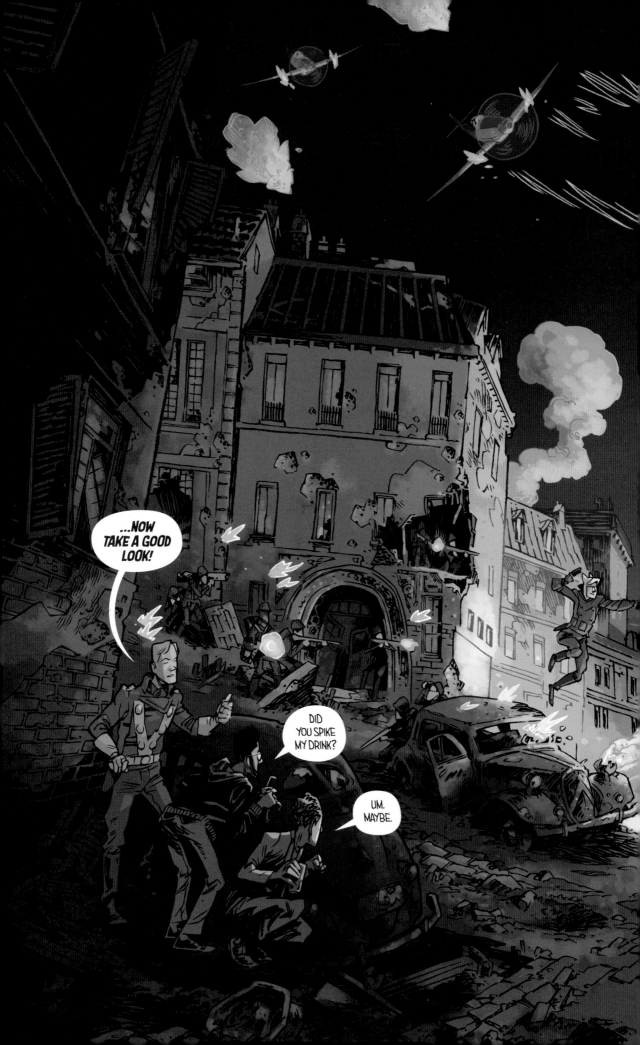

CHAPTER 3

AIRBOY

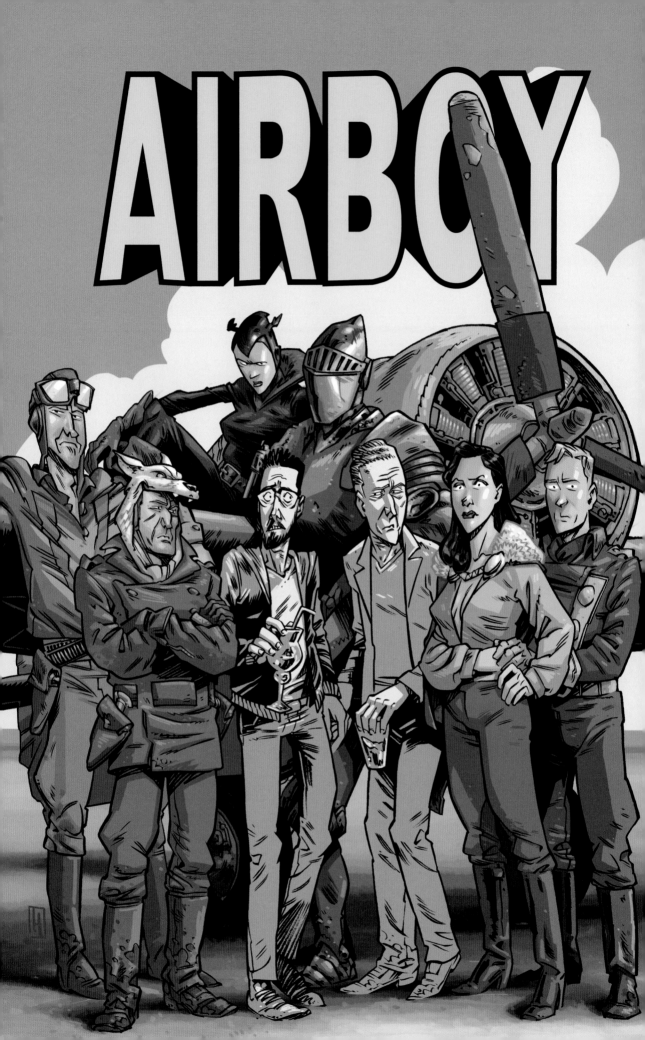

IS THIS REAL?
THIS CAN'T BE REAL.
I MEAN--
WE TOOK DRUGS.
JAMES, TELL ME THIS IS THE DRUGS!
I... I CAN'T SAY THAT IT IS, GREG, NOT WITH CONVICTION.
I'VE DONE LOTS OF DRUGS. LOTS. AND...

...AND IT'S **NEVER** BEEN LIKE THIS!

OH, SO NOW I'VE GOT YOUR ATTENTION.
ERR. WELL, YEAH, OF COURSE YOU HAVE.
IT'S LIKE WORLD WAR 2 IF IT WAS SCIENCE FICTION...
...EXCEPT IT DOESN'T FEEL LIKE SCIENCE FICTION. FEELS REAL.
THE NOISES. ALL THE MACHINE GUN FIRE AND EXPLOSIONS. THE YELLS AND SCREAMS. IT'S ALL AROUND.
THIS IS *WAR*, GENTLEMEN. NOTHING GLAMOROUS ABOUT IT.
AND THE SMELL OF IRON AND SMOKE--
I HAVE TO SAY, AIRBOY, LOOKING DOWN ON IT FROM THE ROOFTOP...
...IT WAS SCARY IN THE STREET, BUT NOW WE'RE UP HIGH AND SAFE...
...IT IS KIND OF GLAMOROUS.
YOU'RE AN IDIOT.
WELL I ADMIT THAT...
...BUT DOWN THERE... ARE STEAM-PUNK **BATTLE SUITS**! WE HAVE *NOTHING* LIKE THAT IN OUR WORLD.
LIKE *MIGNOLA* WOULD DRAW.
YES, WELL I BET THIS MIG-*NOLA* GUY ISN'T DEPRAVED LIKE YOU TWO CLOWNS AND TELLS STORIES WITH DECENCY.

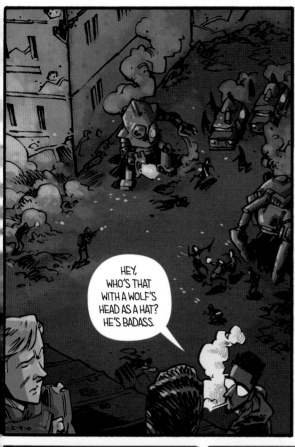

HEY, WHO'S THAT WITH A WOLF'S HEAD AS A HAT? HE'S BADASS.

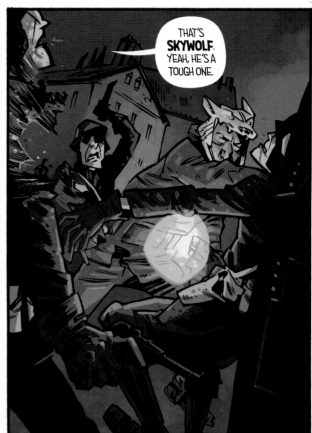

THAT'S **SKYWOLF**. YEAH, HE'S A TOUGH ONE.

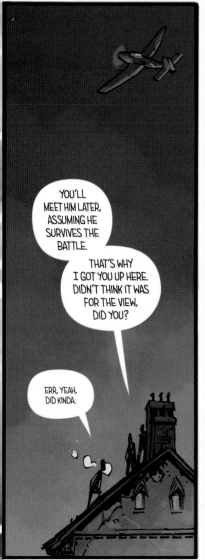

YOU'LL MEET HIM LATER, ASSUMING HE SURVIVES THE BATTLE.

THAT'S WHY I GOT YOU UP HERE. DIDN'T THINK IT WAS FOR THE VIEW, DID YOU?

ERR, YEAH, DID KINDA.

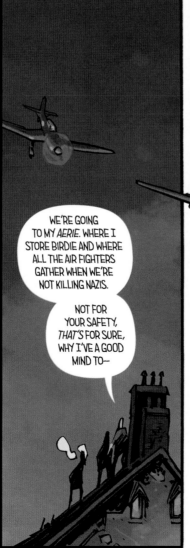

WE'RE GOING TO MY *AERIE*, WHERE I STORE BIRDIE AND WHERE ALL THE AIR FIGHTERS GATHER WHEN WE'RE NOT KILLING NAZIS.

NOT FOR YOUR SAFETY, *THAT'S* FOR SURE, WHY I'VE A GOOD MIND TO—

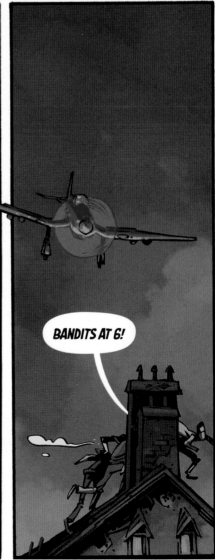

BANDITS AT 6!

MOVE IT!

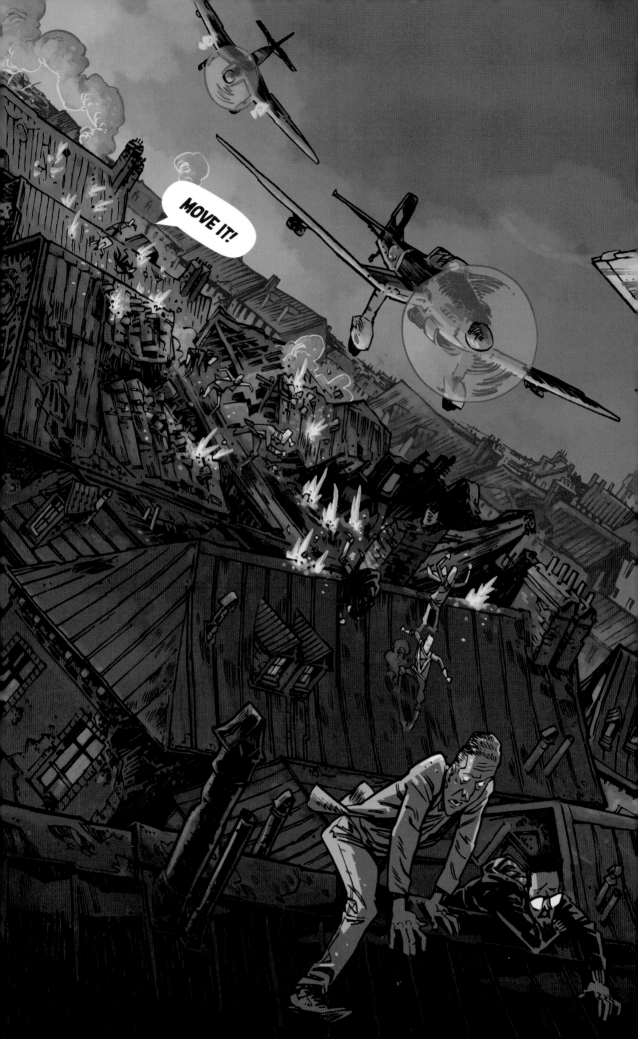

THAT WAS THE MOST EXCITING THING I'VE EVER EXPERIENCED!
I THINK I JUST CAME.
WELL, I KNOW THAT I MADE.
LOOK, I'M STILL AS HARD AS ALL GET OUT.
WAIT, BACK UP. WHAT DID YOU JUST SAY?
AS IN... I SHAT MYSELF.
SNIFF SNIFF
OH YEAH, YOU'RE NOT JOKING.
LOVELY...
BRAVO FOR KEEPING IT CLASSY, GENTLEMEN.

NOW, IF YOU AND *STINKY* HURRY ON UP...
I'M AN AIR FIGHTER. SIMPLE.
YOU SEEMED SO YOUNG AND NAIVE IN SAN FRANCISCO, NOW YOU'RE... ERR... I DON'T EVEN KNOW QUITE HOW TO DESCRIBE IT. MORE THAN JUST CONFIDENT NOW WHERE YOU WEREN'T BEFORE. YOU'RE--
HEY, AIRBOY, YOU'VE **CHANGED**. YOU'RE NOT UNSURE OR--
BUT I DO NOTICE--
I HAVE NO IDEA.
WHAT DOES THAT EVEN MEAN?
I'VE MET GYPSY FORTUNE TELLERS WHO MADE MORE SENSE THAN YOU TWO.
COME ON, GUYS.
OR *YOU'RE* IN *MY* HEAD, *SAYING* THAT I'M IN YOUR HEAD.
YEAH, BUT I'M IN IT. *I'M* NOT IN *YOUR* HEAD. I'M HERE TOO.
I LOVE *ASSASSIN'S CREED*, SO I THINK THIS IS JUST ME DREAMING *THIS* US IN MY HEAD.
FOLLOW ME.
THIS IS CRAZY. *SUPER* COMPLICATED.
THIS IS LIKE *ASSASSIN'S CREED*, ALL CLIMBING AND JUMPING AND WORKING OUT HOW TO GET FROM POINT A TO POINT B.
YEAH, IT'S WHY I THINK WE'RE TRIPPING.

...YOU CAN MEET THE REST OF US.
I'LL MAKE THE INTRODUCTIONS BRIEF.
THIS IS THE GUY YOU SAW FIGHTING IN THE STREET EARLIER...
...SKYWOLF.
JEEZ, DAVE, WHERE THE HELL DID YOU FIND THESE TWO CHARLIES?

THIS IS THE **FLYING DUTCHMAN**.
YEAH, THEY LOOK LIKE HOBOS.
THIS IS THE **IRON ACE.**
SYLVIA MANNERS, THE **BLACK ANGEL**.
NOT WISHING TO BE *RUDE*, BUT I AGREE THEY DO LOOK UNSAVORY. ARE YOU SURE IT WAS THE SMARTEST THING BRINGING THEM HERE?
HMPH.
AND THE OTHER LADY OF THE HOUSE... ERR... HEY, WHERE'S VAL?

OVER HERE, YOU HORSE'S ASS.
GUYS, THIS IS MY GIRL LIS-- LISELLOTTE VON SCHELLENDORF'S HER FULL NAME-- BIT OF A MOUTHFUL, HUH?
MOST EVERYONE SIMPLY CALLS HER **VALKYRIE**.
WHERE HAVE YOU BEEN? I'M **FURIOUS** WITH YOU!
VAL, *BABY*, I HAD NO CONTROL OVER WHAT HAPPENED-- UHH-- HOLD ON--
HEY, FELLAS, COULD ME AND VAL HAVE A MOMENT TO OURSELVES?

WHAT DID HE DO?
WHO KNOWS? SOMETIMES *SHE* ISN'T HAPPY WITH HIM, SOMETIMES *HE* ISN'T HAPPY WITH HER.
IT'S A SEE-SAW.
YEAH, AND WE'RE CAUGHT IN THE MIDDLE HAVIN' TO LISTEN TO THEIR CRAP. GIVE ME NAZIS ANY DAY.
DON'T GET THE REFERENCE, CHUM...
WELL, THAT'S A T-SHIRT.
SLAP
OUCH.
DAVEY LIKES WILD WOMEN. BUT HE AIN'T SUITED TO 'EM.
AMEN TO THAT.
SO, ARE THEY EVER HAPPY?
YOU KNOW, I THINK THE ONLY TIME I'VE SEEN THEM BOTH TRULY HAPPY...
...IS WHEN THEY'RE IN THE AIR.

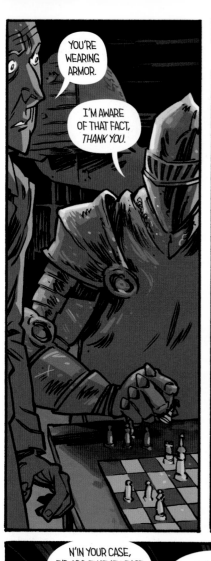

YOU'RE WEARING ARMOR.

I'M AWARE OF THAT FACT, *THANK YOU*.

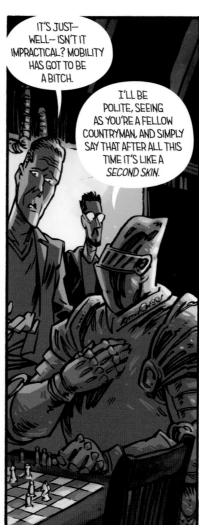

IT'S JUST— WELL— ISN'T IT IMPRACTICAL? MOBILITY HAS GOT TO BE A BITCH.

I'LL BE POLITE, SEEING AS YOU'RE A FELLOW COUNTRYMAN, AND SIMPLY SAY THAT AFTER ALL THIS TIME IT'S LIKE A *SECOND SKIN*.

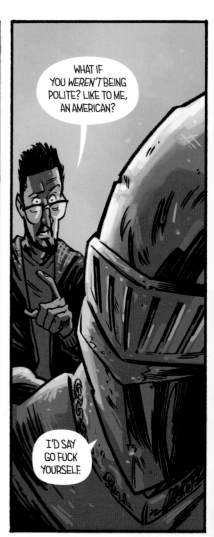

WHAT IF YOU *WEREN'T* BEING POLITE? LIKE TO ME, AN AMERICAN?

I'D SAY GO FUCK YOURSELF.

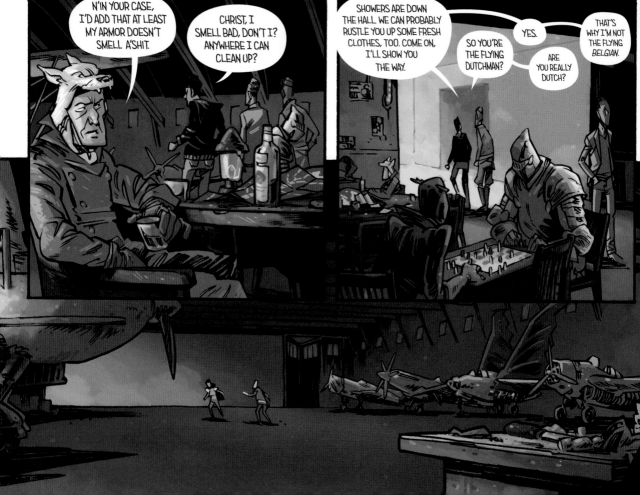

N'IN YOUR CASE, I'D ADD THAT AT LEAST MY ARMOR DOESN'T SMELL A'SHIT.

CHRIST, I SMELL BAD, DON'T I? ANYWHERE I CAN CLEAN UP?

SHOWERS ARE DOWN THE HALL. WE CAN PROBABLY RUSTLE YOU UP SOME FRESH CLOTHES, TOO. COME ON, I'LL SHOW YOU THE WAY.

SO YOU'RE THE FLYING DUTCHMAN?

YES.

ARE YOU REALLY DUTCH?

THAT'S WHY I'M NOT THE FLYING *BELGIAN*.

WELL, THAT WAS EMBARASSING FOR YOU TO SEE.
NO, IT'S-- I FOUND IT REASSURING, SORT OF, THE FACT THAT HERE-- WHEREVER *THIS* IS, ANOTHER DIMENSION OR JUST A DREAM IN MY HEAD-- THAT THINGS BETWEEN THE SEXES ARE AS FUCKED UP AS THEY ARE IN MY REALITY.
DAVID, CAN WE WALK? MAY WE, I SHOULD SAY.
SOMETHING IN MY GUT IS MAKING ME WANT TO LOOK AROUND.
SURE, I BROUGHT YOU HERE, SO THAT MEANS YOU'RE MY GUEST.
THIS IS OUR MAIN HALL.
WE HANG OUT HERE, EAT, DRINK, MAINTAIN OUR AIRCRAFT. BIT OF EVERYTHING.
AND THE NAZIS DON'T SPOT THIS PLACE HOW, EXACTLY? PRETTY VISIBLE TO ME.
SOME LIGHT TRICK. LENSES. "LIGHT REFRACTION," SYLVIA? THAT'S WHAT YOU CALLED IT, RIGHT?
THAT'S CORRECT, DAVEY.
SHE STOLE IT FROM SOME GERMAN SCIENTIST. LENSES PROJECT A DIFFERENT VIEW TO THE GERMANS...
TO THEM WE'RE A BIG, BURNED OUT SKELETON.
OH. COOL.
WHAT'S THROUGH HERE?
BEDROOMS.
KITCHEN.
MORGUE.
HUH.

WAIT, WHAT?
YOU HAVE A MORGUE?
SOLDIERS DIE, JAMES. FRIENDS AND BROTHERS-IN-ARMS. WE'RE NOT ABOUT TO LEAVE THEM TO ROT IN THE STREET.
COUPLE OF AIR FIGHTERS WHO BOUGHT THE FARM--
--BLACK COMMANDER AND THE BALD EAGLE--
-- ALONG WITH A LOT OF ALLIED SOLDIERS.
I WANT TO SEE.
YOU SURE? IT'S NOT A FUN PLACE.
ABSOLUTELY... YOU KNOW I SAID I HAD THE URGE TO LOOK AROUND...
...WELL THAT URGE IS DRAWING ME THERE.
SEE. LOTS OF DRAWERS. LOTS OF BODIES.

HERE.
I HAVE A CRAZY **NEED** SUDDENLY TO KNOW WHO'S IN THAT DRAWER.
SAYS HE'S BRITISH. HE'S-- HEY, SAME NAME AS YOU.
LET ME SEE. OPEN IT.
WOW, THAT *IS* YOU!
YOUNGER AND BLOWN TO SHIT, BUT YEAH, IT SURE LOOKS LIKE ME.
AGAIN, DAVID, I DON'T KNOW WHAT THIS IS. IF IT'S **DRUGS** OR **DREAMS** OR IF WE'VE ENTERED ANOTHER **DIMENSION**, BUT...
...IN *THIS* REALITY, I DIED.
WHAT ARE YOU DOING?
LOOKING FOR ANYTHING HE MAY HAVE HAD ON HIM.
YEAH, WALLET.
HE HAD A SWEET-HEART.
NO, HE HAD A WIFE...
XOXO
...THAT'S JANN. I'M MARRIED TO HER IN MY WORLD, TOO.

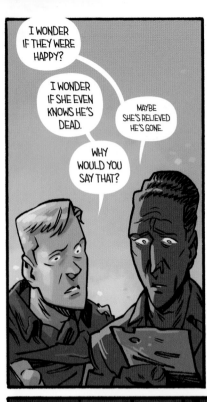

I WONDER IF THEY WERE HAPPY?

I WONDER IF SHE EVEN KNOWS HE'S DEAD.

MAYBE SHE'S RELIEVED HE'S GONE.

WHY WOULD YOU SAY THAT?

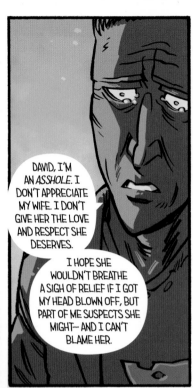

DAVID, I'M AN *ASSHOLE*. I DON'T APPRECIATE MY WIFE. I DON'T GIVE HER THE LOVE AND RESPECT SHE DESERVES.

I HOPE SHE WOULDN'T BREATHE A SIGH OF RELIEF IF I GOT MY HEAD BLOWN OFF, BUT PART OF ME SUSPECTS SHE MIGHT—AND I CAN'T BLAME HER.

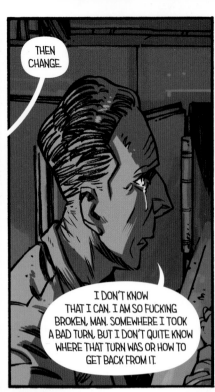

THEN CHANGE.

I DON'T KNOW THAT I CAN. I AM SO FUCKING BROKEN, MAN. SOMEWHERE I TOOK A BAD TURN, BUT I DON'T QUITE KNOW WHERE THAT TURN WAS OR HOW TO GET BACK FROM IT.

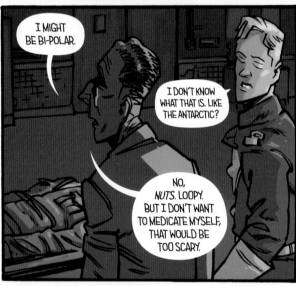

I MIGHT BE BI-POLAR.

I DON'T KNOW WHAT THAT IS. LIKE THE ANTARCTIC?

NO, *NUTS*. LOOPY. BUT I DON'T WANT TO MEDICATE MYSELF, THAT WOULD BE TOO SCARY.

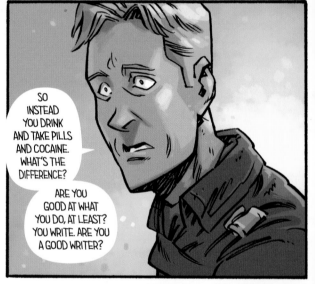

SO INSTEAD YOU DRINK AND TAKE PILLS AND COCAINE. WHAT'S THE DIFFERENCE?

ARE YOU GOOD AT WHAT YOU DO, AT LEAST? YOU WRITE. ARE YOU A GOOD WRITER?

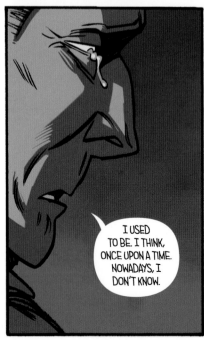

I USED TO BE. I THINK, ONCE UPON A TIME. NOWADAYS, I DON'T KNOW.

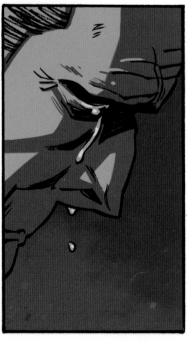

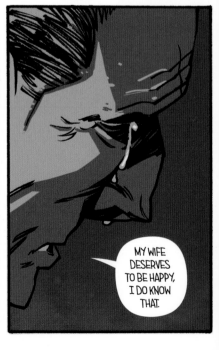

MY WIFE DESERVES TO BE HAPPY, I DO KNOW THAT.

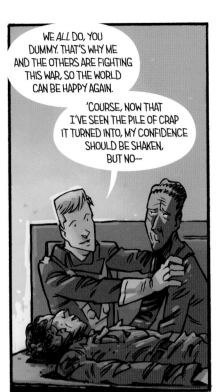

WE *ALL* DO, YOU DUMMY. THAT'S WHY ME AND THE OTHERS ARE FIGHTING THIS WAR, SO THE WORLD CAN BE HAPPY AGAIN.

'COURSE, NOW THAT I'VE SEEN THE PILE OF CRAP IT TURNED INTO, MY CONFIDENCE SHOULD BE SHAKEN, BUT NO—

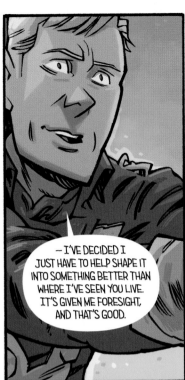

—I'VE DECIDED I JUST HAVE TO HELP SHAPE IT INTO SOMETHING BETTER THAN WHERE I'VE SEEN YOU LIVE. IT'S GIVEN ME FORESIGHT, AND THAT'S GOOD.

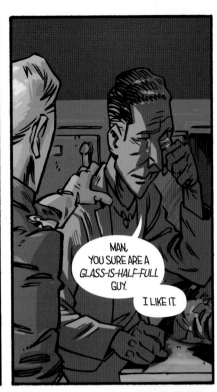

MAN, YOU SURE ARE A *GLASS-IS-HALF-FULL* GUY.

I LIKE IT.

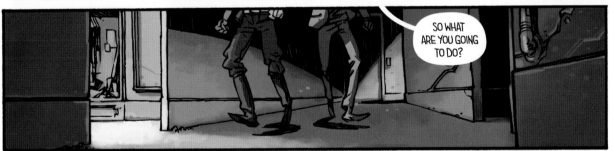

SO WHAT'S GOING ON WITH YOU AND VALKYRIE?

WE'RE... ERR... LITTLE THINGS BECOME BIG THINGS WITH HER AND ME. BUT I CAN'T LET HER GO. I LOVE HER.

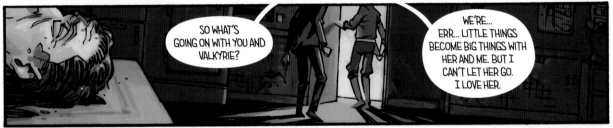

SO WHAT ARE YOU GOING TO DO?

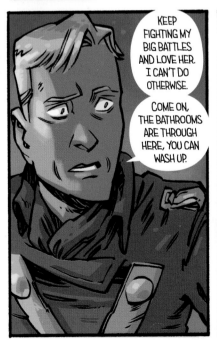

KEEP FIGHTING MY BIG BATTLES AND LOVE HER. I CAN'T DO OTHERWISE.

COME ON, THE BATHROOMS ARE THROUGH HERE, YOU CAN WASH UP.

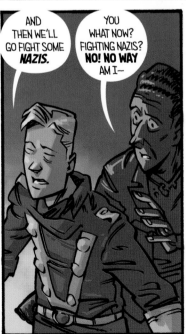

AND THEN WE'LL GO FIGHT SOME *NAZIS.*

YOU WHAT NOW? FIGHTING NAZIS? **NO! NO WAY** AM I—

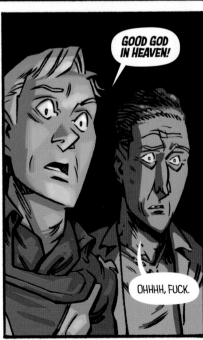

GOOD GOD IN HEAVEN!

OHHHH, FUCK.

GREG!
NOT GOOD.
VAL!
YES? WHAT?
VAL, HOW COULD YOU?
YOU DESERVED IT! YOU VANISHED AND I WAS SCARED SILLY THAT YOU WERE DEAD.
SO YOU HAD SEX WITH THIS JOKER? HOW IS THAT FAIR?
FAIR? FAIR? I'M A FREE SPIRIT, DAVEY, AND ALWAYS HAVE BEEN. I MAKE MY OWN RULES.
YOU NEEDED A LESSON, SO I GOT THE MOST DISGUSTING, REPULSIVE MAN I COULD FIND.
AIRBOY, I DON'T KNOW WHAT CAME OVER ME -- WAIT, I'M "REPULSIVE"?
GREG, STOP TALKING, YOU'VE CAUSED ENOUGH MESS.
YEAH...

...SHUT UP, GREG!
SOK
WHAT'S GOING ON!
THIS BASTARD JUST MADE LOVE TO VAL.
OH NO, DAVID, IT WASN'T LOVE...
...IT WAS CARNAL!
BOY, YOU GOT YOUR HANDS FULL WITH THAT ONE.
YOU CAN SHUT UP, TOO.
WOW, LOOK AT THAT GUY, HE'S HUGE! BETWEEN HIS LEGS I MEAN.
YEAH, HUNG LIKE A CAMEL.
GUYS, YOU'RE NOT HELPING.
ALL RIGHT, THIS IS THE SECOND TIME YOU APES HAVE GOTTEN ME MAD--
WAIT, WHAT DID I DO?
WE HAVE A MISSION. IMPORTANT TO THE WAR...

A BRIDGE THAT NEEDS DESTROYING.
WE — THE AIR FIGHTERS — WERE GOING TO MAKE AN ASSAULT IN A FEW HOURS, 'CEPT *WE'RE* NOT ANYMORE...

...YOU ARE!
GULP.

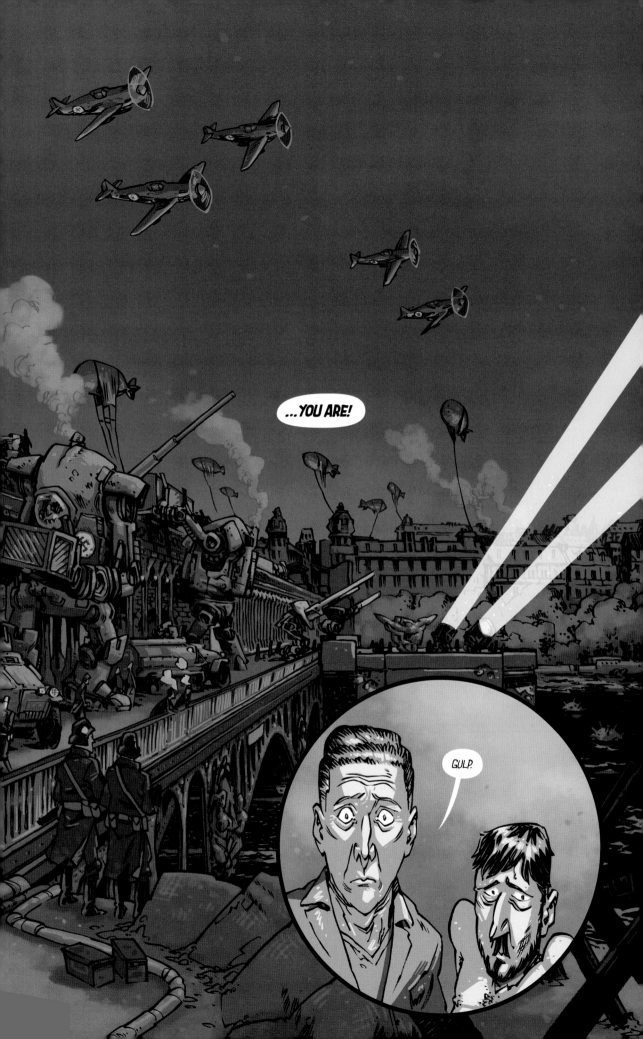

CHAPTER 4

CAFE

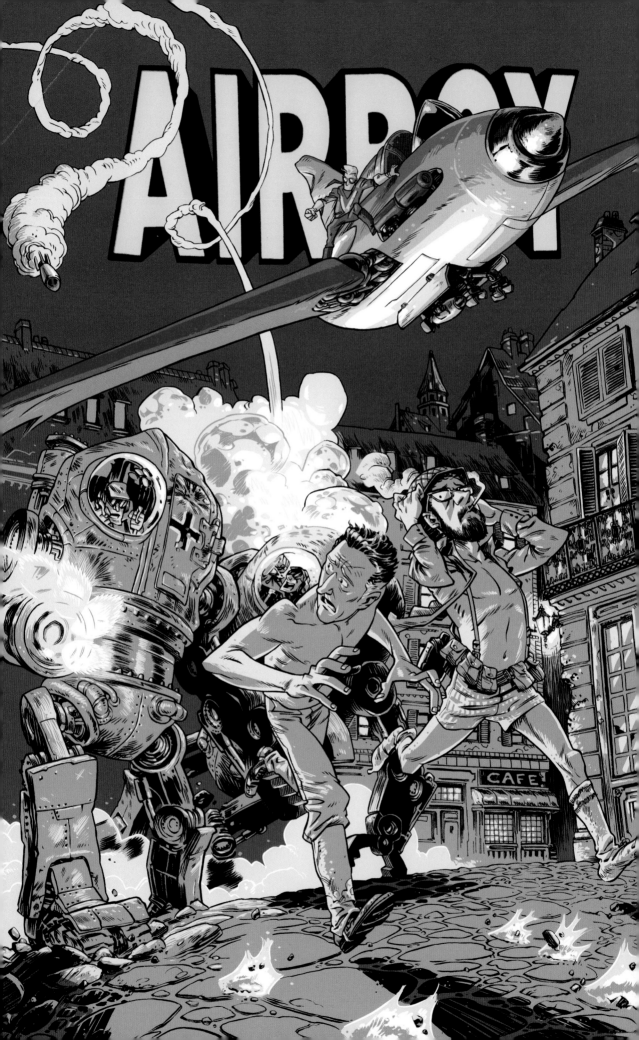

I FEEL BAD.

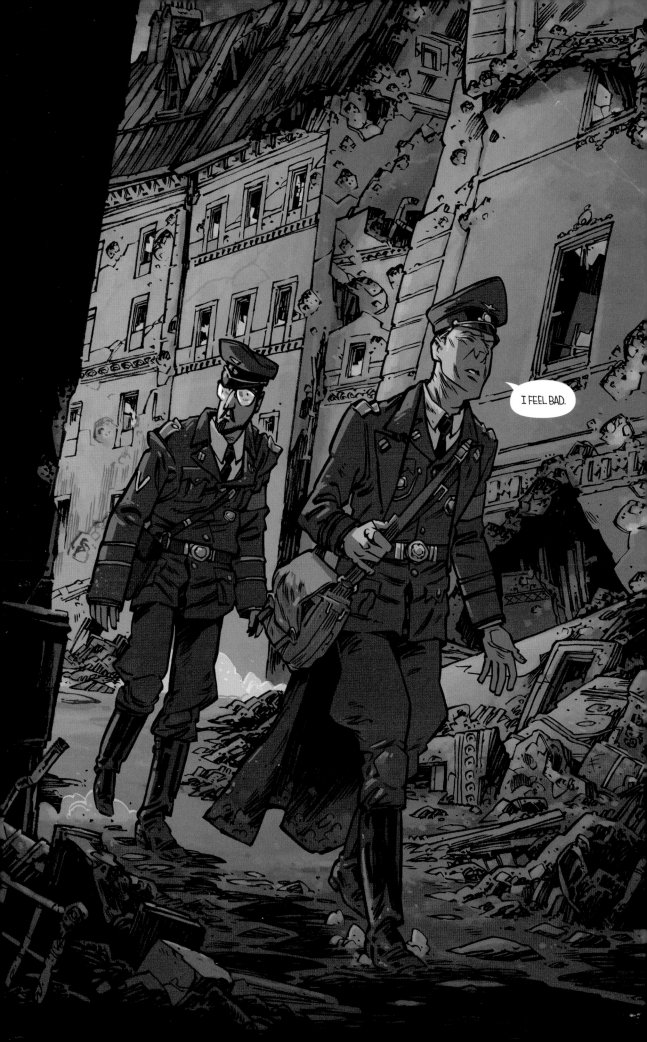

YEAH, IF WE GET CAUGHT WITH THESE UNIFORMS ON, IT'LL BE REAL BAD.
NO, ME. I *FEEL* BAD.
SICK?
I FORGIVE YOU.
SO, WHY DO YOU FEEL BAD?
I FEEL GUILTY. I KNOW WE'RE IN S.S. UNIFORMS, THE MOST VILE AND DESPISED PART OF THE ALREADY VILE AND DESPICABLE NAZI REGIME...
...AND I FEEL FUCKING COOL. THESE UNIFORMS--
LOOK FUCKING COO I KNOW.
WE'RE GETTING CLOSE TO THE GERMANS.
LET'S HOPE YOUR BEARD DOESN'T GIVE US AWAY.
I THINK WITH NEITHER OF US SPEAKING GERMAN, MY *BEARD* IS THE LEAST OF OUR PROBLEMS.
JESUS, WHY DID WE AGREE TO DO THIS?

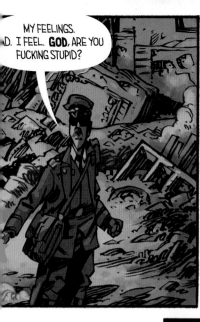

MY FEELINGS. D. I FEEL. **GOD**, ARE YOU FUCKING STUPID?

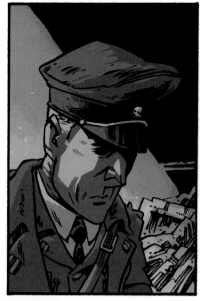

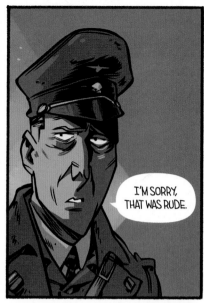

I'M SORRY, THAT WAS RUDE.

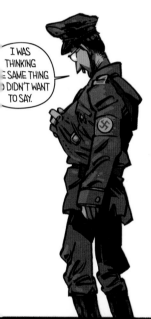

I WAS THINKING E SAME THING D DIDN'T WANT TO SAY.

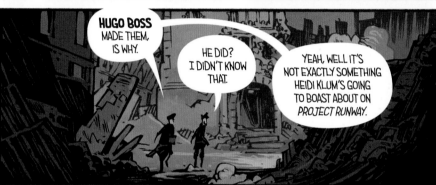

HUGO BOSS MADE THEM, IS WHY.

HE DID? I DIDN'T KNOW THAT.

YEAH, WELL IT'S NOT EXACTLY SOMETHING HEIDI KLUM'S GOING TO BOAST ABOUT ON *PROJECT RUNWAY.*

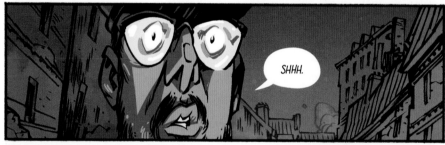

SHHH.

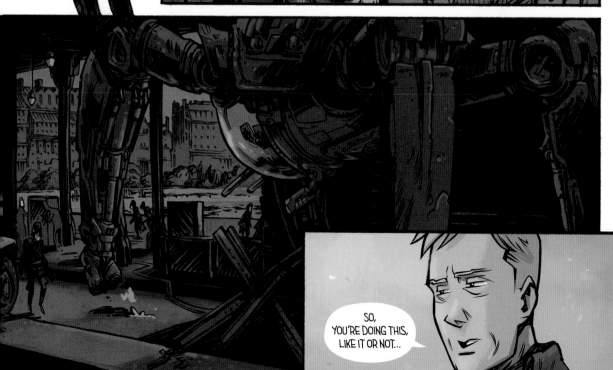

SO, YOU'RE DOING THIS, LIKE IT OR NOT...

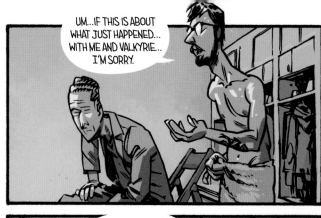

UM...IF THIS IS ABOUT WHAT JUST HAPPENED... WITH ME AND VALKYRIE... I'M SORRY.

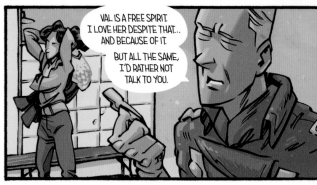

VAL IS A FREE SPIRIT. I LOVE HER DESPITE THAT... AND BECAUSE OF IT.

BUT ALL THE SAME, I'D RATHER NOT TALK TO YOU.

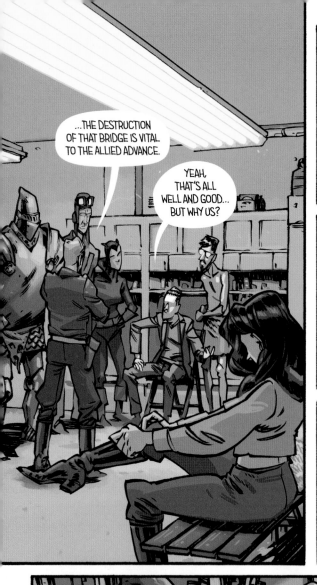

...THE DESTRUCTION OF THAT BRIDGE IS VITAL TO THE ALLIED ADVANCE.

YEAH, THAT'S ALL WELL AND GOOD... BUT WHY US?

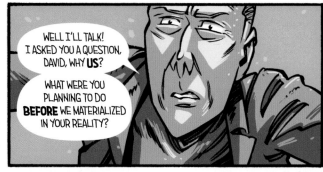

WELL I'LL TALK! I ASKED YOU A QUESTION, DAVID, WHY **US**?

WHAT WERE YOU PLANNING TO DO **BEFORE** WE MATERIALIZED IN YOUR REALITY?

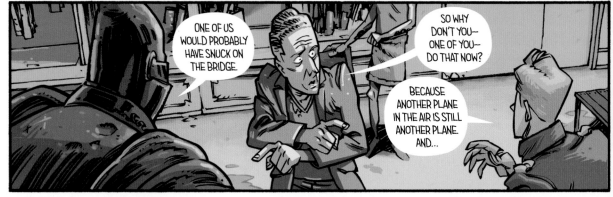

ONE OF US WOULD PROBABLY HAVE SNUCK ON THE BRIDGE.

SO WHY DON'T YOU— ONE OF YOU— DO THAT NOW?

BECAUSE ANOTHER PLANE IN THE AIR IS STILL ANOTHER PLANE. AND...

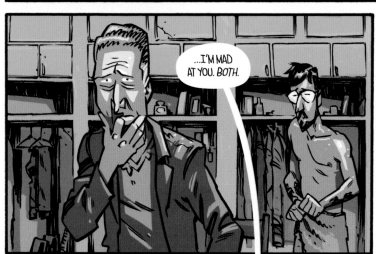

...I'M MAD AT YOU. *BOTH.*

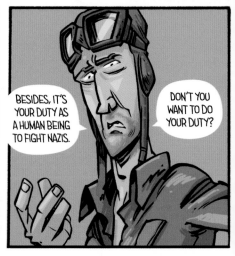

BESIDES, IT'S YOUR DUTY AS A HUMAN BEING TO FIGHT NAZIS.

DON'T YOU WANT TO DO YOUR DUTY?

IT'S JUST A **FANTASY**, JAMES. ALL OF THIS, AND **DON'T** FORGET THAT.
AN ADVENTUROUS **DREAM**.
WE UNDERTAKE THIS AND WE DO GET KILLED, WE'LL JUST WAKE UP.
OR WE'LL HAVE A HEART ATTACK OR A STROKE IN OUR SLEEP OR SOMETHING-- THIS IS ALL TOO **REAL**-- I MEAN...
...I MEAN, DOES THIS FEEL LIKE "JUST A DREAM"?
I NEED TO THINK.

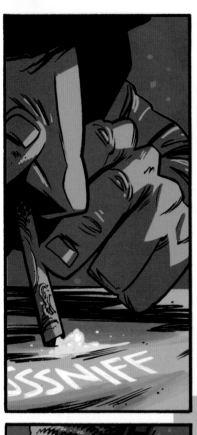

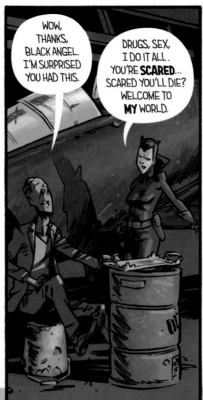

WOW, THANKS, BLACK ANGEL. I'M SURPRISED YOU HAD THIS.

DRUGS, SEX, I DO IT ALL. YOU'RE **SCARED**... SCARED YOU'LL DIE? WELCOME TO **MY** WORLD.

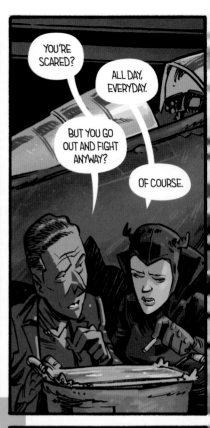

YOU'RE SCARED?

ALL DAY, EVERYDAY.

BUT YOU GO OUT AND FIGHT ANYWAY?

OF COURSE.

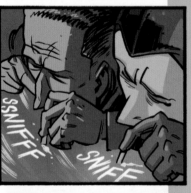

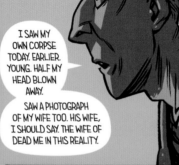

I SAW MY OWN CORPSE TODAY. EARLIER. YOUNG. HALF MY HEAD BLOWN AWAY.

SAW A PHOTOGRAPH OF MY WIFE TOO. HIS WIFE, I SHOULD SAY. THE WIFE OF DEAD ME IN THIS REALITY.

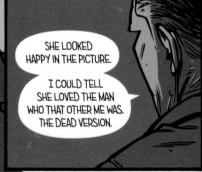

SHE LOOKED HAPPY IN THE PICTURE.

I COULD TELL SHE LOVED THE MAN WHO THAT OTHER ME WAS. THE DEAD VERSION.

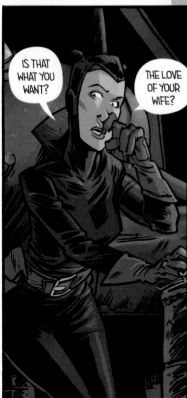

IS THAT WHAT YOU WANT?

THE LOVE OF YOUR WIFE?

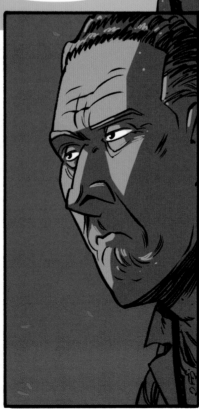

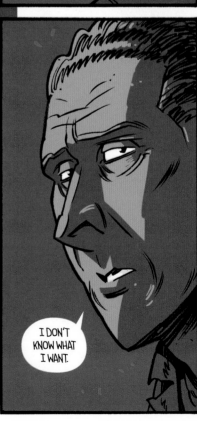

I DON'T KNOW WHAT I WANT.

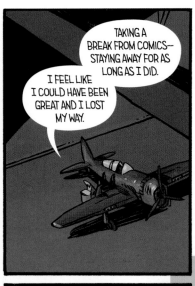

TAKING A BREAK FROM COMICS—STAYING AWAY FOR AS LONG AS I DID.

I FEEL LIKE I COULD HAVE BEEN GREAT AND I LOST MY WAY.

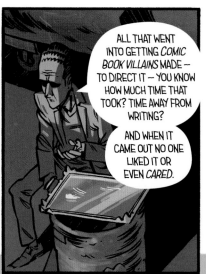

ALL THAT WENT INTO GETTING *COMIC BOOK VILLAINS* MADE — TO DIRECT IT — YOU KNOW HOW MUCH TIME THAT TOOK? TIME AWAY FROM WRITING?

AND WHEN IT CAME OUT NO ONE LIKED IT OR EVEN *CARED*.

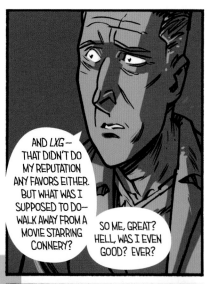

AND *LXG*— THAT DIDN'T DO MY REPUTATION ANY FAVORS EITHER. BUT WHAT WAS I SUPPOSED TO DO— WALK AWAY FROM A MOVIE STARRING CONNERY?

SO ME, GREAT? HELL, WAS I EVEN GOOD? EVER?

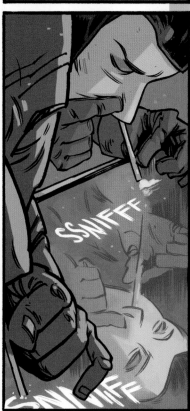

SSNIFFF

SSNIFFF

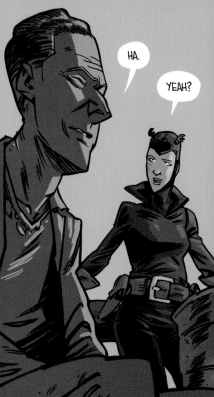

HA.

YEAH?

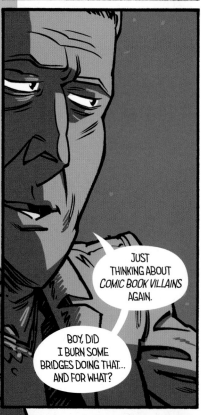

JUST THINKING ABOUT *COMIC BOOK VILLAINS* AGAIN.

BOY, DID I BURN SOME BRIDGES DOING THAT... AND FOR WHAT?

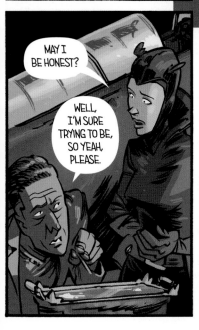

MAY I BE HONEST?

WELL, I'M SURE TRYING TO BE, SO YEAH, PLEASE.

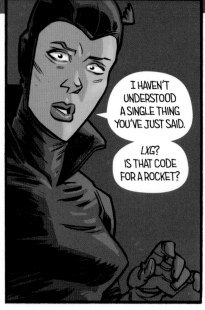

I HAVEN'T UNDERSTOOD A SINGLE THING YOU'VE JUST SAID.

LXG? IS THAT CODE FOR A ROCKET?

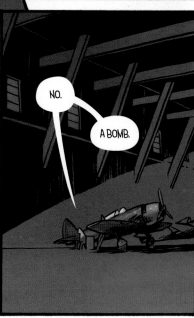

NO.

A BOMB.

WELL, ALL I KNOW IS THE ONLY PEOPLE WHO TRULY AREN'T GREAT ARE THE ONES WHO'VE GIVEN UP TRYING TO BE.
AND SOMETIMES BRIDGES NEED BURNING.
I CAN THINK OF ONE BRIDGE WE COULD ALL BURN TOGETHER.
HEY GREG!...
COME ON, LET'S DO THIS!
LET'S BE COMIC BOOK HEROES!

SO IT'S SIMPLE.
SIMPLE? I DOUBT IT.
YOU JUST HAVE TO GET TO WHERE THE EXPLOSIVES ARE PLANTED.
THEY'RE ALREADY ON THE BRIDGE? THEN WHY DIDN'T YOU BLOW IT WHEN YOU HAD THE CHANCE?
IT WASN'T THE RIGHT TIME -- THE RIGHT DAY -- TROOP MOVEMENTS--
OR AS I LIKE TO PUT IT -- DON'T ASK QUESTIONS, SHUT THE FUCK UP AND LISTEN.
OK.
YOU'LL BE WEARING GERMAN UNIFORMS-- OFFICERS -- SO AS LONG AS YOU WALK WITH AUTHORITY AND KEEP TO THE SHADOWS WHERE YOU CAN...
...YOU SHOULD GET TO WHERE YOU'RE GOING WITHOUT ANY TROUBLE.

WHAT HAPPENS IF WE'RE STOPPED, WE START SHOOTING?
HAVE YOU EVER SHOT ANYONE?
NO.
THEN NO GUNS FOR YOU, YOU'LL END UP SHOOTING YOURSELVES MORE THAN LIKELY. SEEN IT HAPPEN.
WE'LL BE IN THE AIR BY THEN ANYWAY...

...ALL OF US.

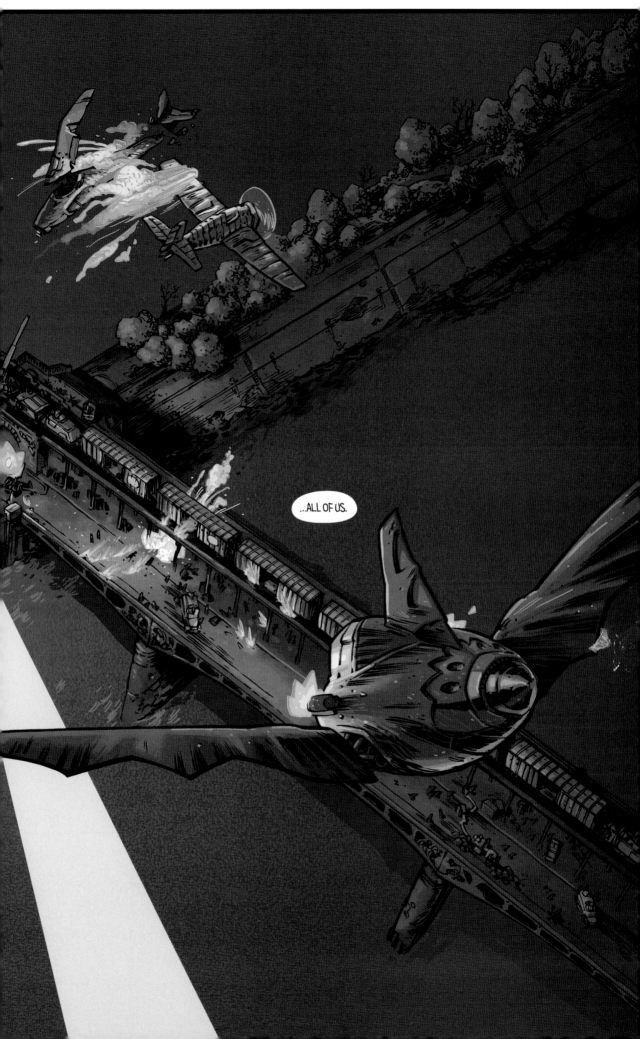

WE'LL DRAW THE GERMAN'S FIRE AND ATTENTION AWAY FROM YOU.
YOU ACTIVATE THE EXPLOSIVE'S TIMER AND GET OFF THE BRIDGE.
YOU KNOW...
...THAT ACTUALLY IS A PRETTY SIMPLE PLAN.
SO ANY QUESTIONS? ANYTHING, YOU'D LIKE TO SAY...
...BEFORE WE START OUR ENGINES?
I WANT TO SAY THIS, AIRBOY. SOMETHING I'VE BEEN TRYING TO SAY FROM THE START, BUT WELL—
I DON'T KNOW IF THIS IS A DREAM OR NOT, BUT I'M ALRIGHT WITH IT. THE AIR FIGHTER, AVIATION PART OF IT ANYWAY. MY DAD WORKED FOR AN AIRLINE, I PRACTICALLY GREW UP AT THE AIRPORT. WE GOT TO FLY FOR FREE, SO EVERY HOLIDAY STARTED AND ENDED WITH A PLANE RIDE. I COULDN'T TELL YOU HOW MANY HOURS I SPENT IN THOSE UNCOMFORTABLE AIRLINE CHAIRS, WATCHING PLANES LAND AND TAKE OFF. TO ME, IT'S NOT CHRISTMAS IF I DON'T SMELL JET FUEL AND BURNING RUBBER.
SO WHATEVER THIS IS, DREAM OR KARMIC RETRIBUTION, I'M LOVING IT. AND IF WE DIE TODAY, IF THIS IS MY LAST VACATION, I'M GRATEFUL FOR THE MEMORIES.
OH, JEEZ.
I FORGOT MY U.S. ARMY UNIFORM.
JESUS, THAT WAS THE LAST THING AIRBOY SAID.
I KNOW, I KNOW. I WAS LOOKING FOR UNDERWEAR, IT SLIPPED MY MIND.
SO WHAT ARE WE GOING TO DO?
"WE?" WHY IS IT

YOU KNOW JAMES BY NOW, IF IT'S NOT ABOUT HIM HE'S NOT INTERESTED.
WHAT THE FUCK DOES *THAT* MEAN?
JUST GO GET CHANGED.
OH, AND BEFORE YOU PRIME THE BOMB-- SO YOU DON'T GET SHOT AS SPIES IF YOU'RE CAUGHT-- DON'T FORGET TO TAKE ALONG U.S. ARMY UNIFORMS TO CHANGE INTO.
DON'T LOOK AT ME THAT WAY.
SIGH.
ALL RIGHT...

...LET'S TRY NOT TO FUCK THIS UP.
SO, FLYING DUTCHMAN SAID WHAT AGAIN? TURN THE DIAL THEN PRESS THE BUTTONS?
FUCK, WHY WEREN'T YOU LISTENING?
OR WAS IT PRESS THE BUTTONS AND TURN THE DIAL?
WHY WEREN'T YOU?
MM

OHHH, GREG.
NOT GOOD.
FSSSHHH
THOOM
THAT DID THE TRICK-- VALKYRIE TOO, WHO DID IT-- YOU SEE THAT? BADASS HOW SHE--
FUCK...

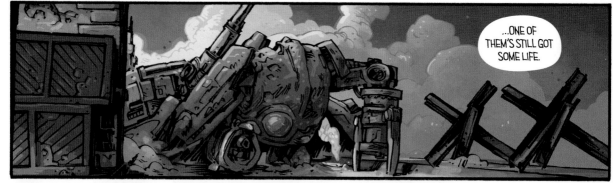

...ONE OF THEM'S STILL GOT SOME LIFE.

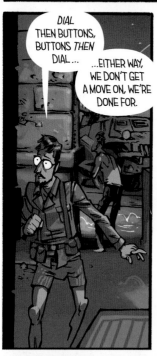

DIAL THEN BUTTONS, BUTTONS *THEN* DIAL...

...EITHER WAY, WE DON'T GET A MOVE ON, WE'RE DONE FOR.

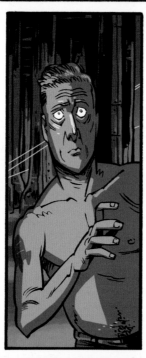

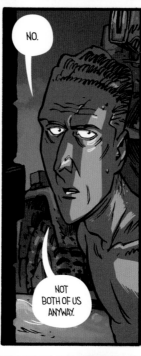

NO.

NOT BOTH OF US ANYWAY.

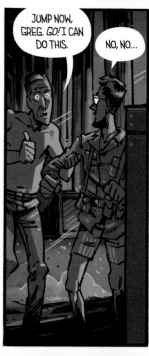

JUMP NOW, GREG. *GO!* I CAN DO THIS.

NO, NO...

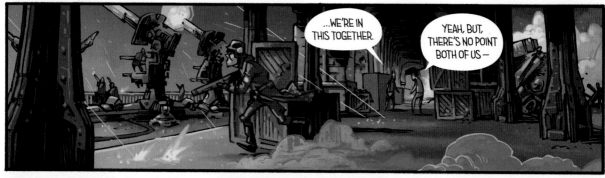

...WE'RE IN THIS TOGETHER.

YEAH, BUT, THERE'S NO POINT BOTH OF US —

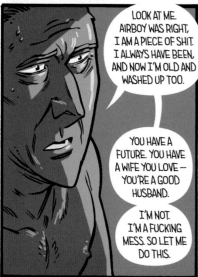

LOOK AT ME. AIRBOY WAS RIGHT, I AM A PIECE OF SHIT. I ALWAYS HAVE BEEN, AND NOW I'M OLD AND WASHED UP TOO.

YOU HAVE A FUTURE. YOU HAVE A WIFE YOU LOVE — YOU'RE A GOOD HUSBAND.

I'M NOT. I'M A FUCKING MESS. SO LET ME DO THIS.

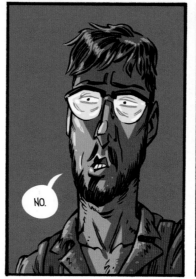

NO.

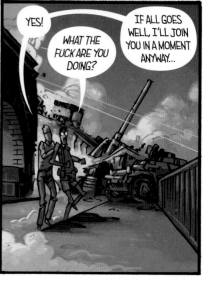

YES!

WHAT THE FUCK ARE YOU DOING?

IF ALL GOES WELL, I'LL JOIN YOU IN A MOMENT ANYWAY...

...SO
OVER THE SIDE
WITH YOU!
HEY,
I HOPE YOU
CAN SWIM.
YOU'RE
A DICK!

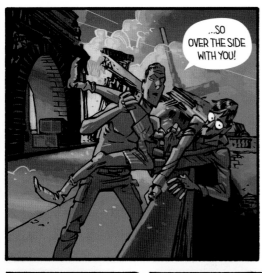

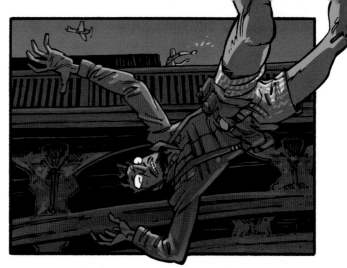

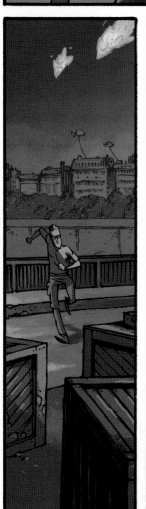

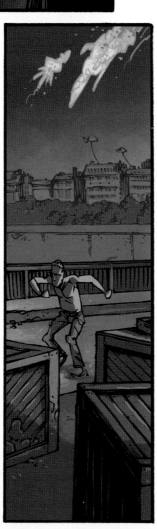

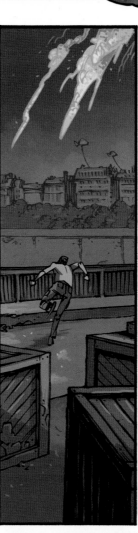

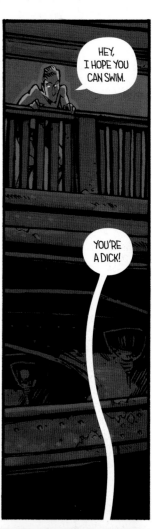

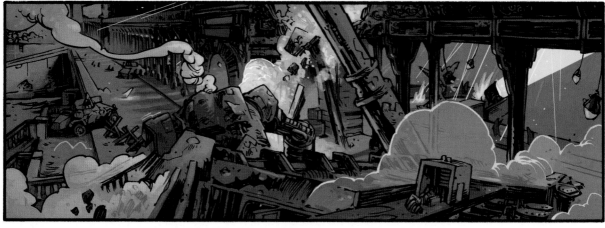

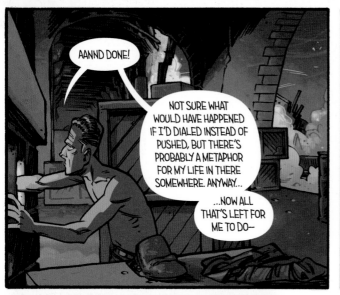

AANND DONE!

NOT SURE WHAT WOULD HAVE HAPPENED IF I'D DIALED INSTEAD OF PUSHED, BUT THERE'S PROBABLY A METAPHOR FOR MY LIFE IN THERE SOMEWHERE. ANYWAY...

...NOW ALL THAT'S LEFT FOR ME TO DO—

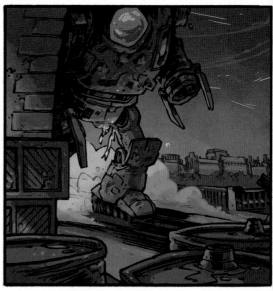

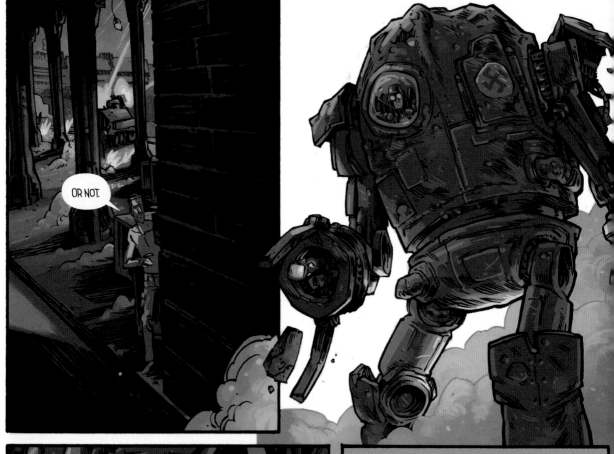

OR NOT.

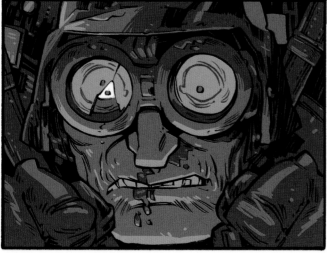

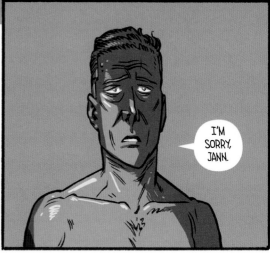

I'M SORRY, JANN.

AIRBOY!
DIDN'T THINK I'D LET YOU DIE, DID YOU?
ERR, YEAH. KINDA DID.

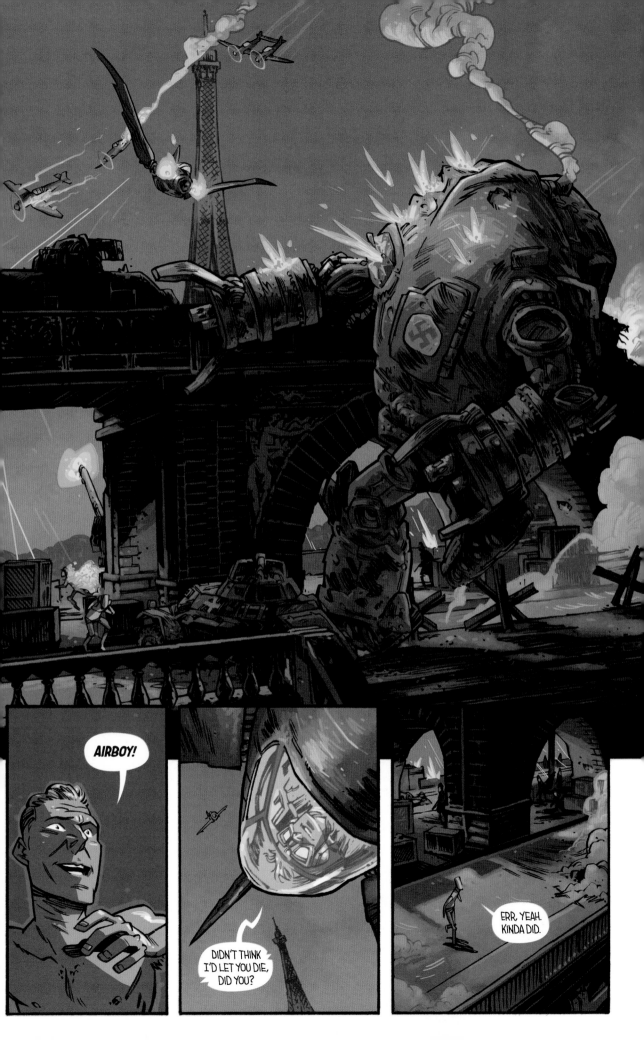

NOW GO! IF THE BOMB'S SET TO BLOW...
...THEN GET OFF THAT BRIDGE...
...AND LIVE YOUR LIFE!
POK
POK

BOOM
WHAT...WHAT...WHAT...
SPLOOSH

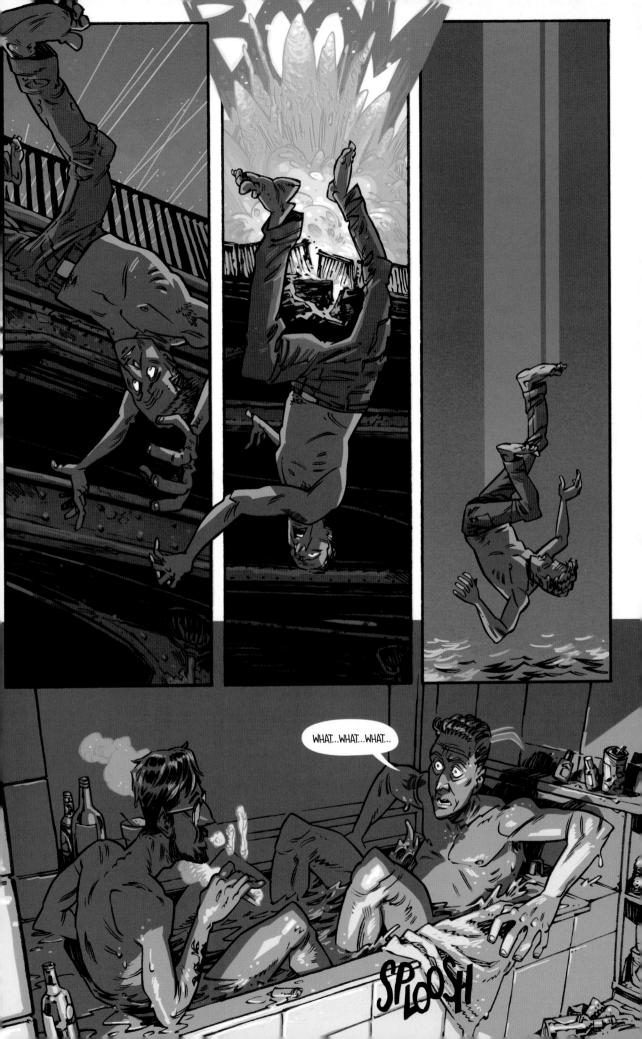

WHERE AM I?
IN THE BATH, GENIUS. BACK AT THE MOTEL. YOU JUST WOKE UP. I ONLY DID A MINUTE BEFORE YOU.
AND AIRBOY?
NO AIRBOY.
SO WE'LL NEVER KNOW.
NO. NOW, HUNGOVER AND WITH OUR HEADS ACHING--*MINE SURE IS ANYWAY*-- I THINK WE CAN BOTH AGREE ... THAT IT NEVER HAPPENED.
SOMETHING'S RESTING ON MY THIGH-- I CAN FEEL IT.
AND IT'S NOT PART OF *ME*.
AND IT'S NOT THE SOAP.

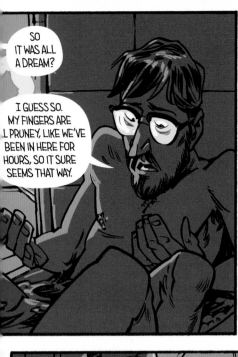

SO IT WAS ALL A DREAM?

I GUESS SO. MY FINGERS ARE LL PRUNEY, LIKE WE'VE BEEN IN HERE FOR HOURS, SO IT SURE SEEMS THAT WAY.

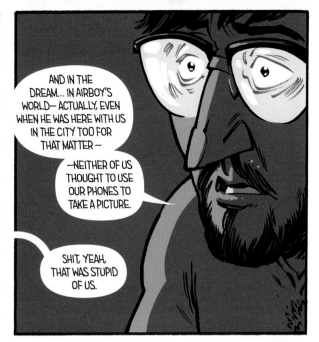

AND IN THE DREAM... IN AIRBOY'S WORLD— ACTUALLY, EVEN WHEN HE WAS HERE WITH US IN THE CITY TOO FOR THAT MATTER —

—NEITHER OF US THOUGHT TO USE OUR PHONES TO TAKE A PICTURE.

SHIT, YEAH, THAT WAS STUPID OF US.

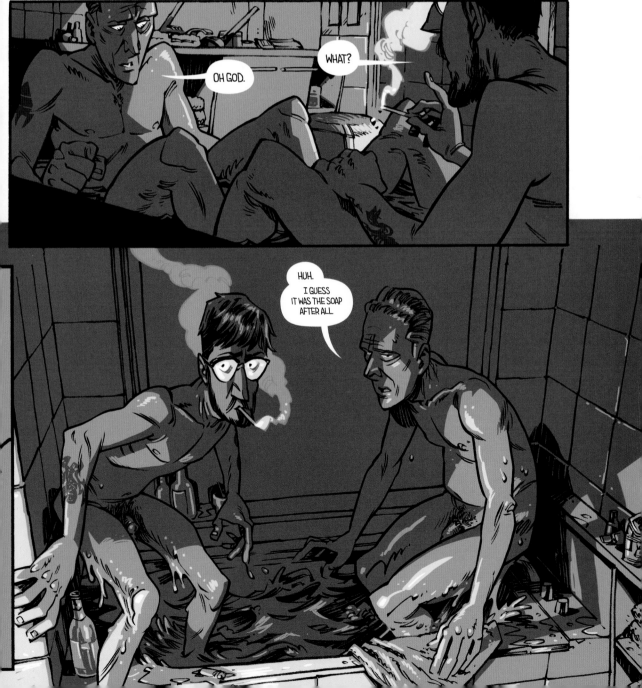

OH GOD.

WHAT?

HUH. I GUESS IT WAS THE SOAP AFTER ALL

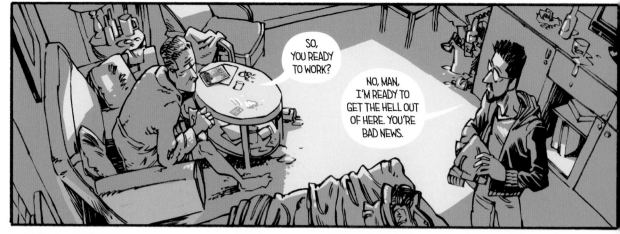

SO, YOU READY TO WORK?

NO, MAN, I'M READY TO GET THE HELL OUT OF HERE. YOU'RE BAD NEWS.

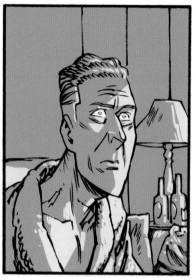

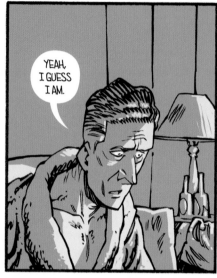

YEAH, I GUESS I AM.

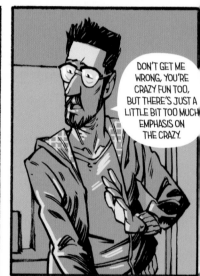

DON'T GET ME WRONG, YOU'RE CRAZY FUN TOO, BUT THERE'S JUST A LITTLE BIT TOO MUCH EMPHASIS ON THE CRAZY.

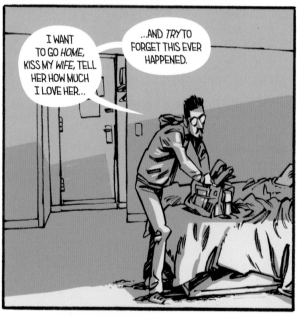

I WANT TO GO *HOME*, KISS MY *WIFE*, TELL HER HOW MUCH I LOVE HER...

...AND *TRY* TO FORGET THIS EVER HAPPENED.

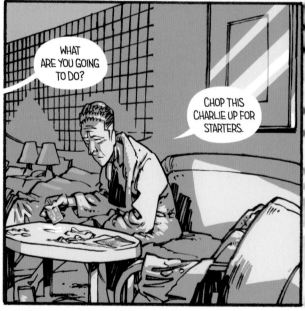

WHAT ARE YOU GOING TO DO?

CHOP THIS CHARLIE UP FOR STARTERS.

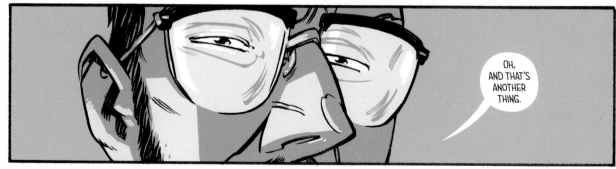

OH, AND THAT'S ANOTHER THING.

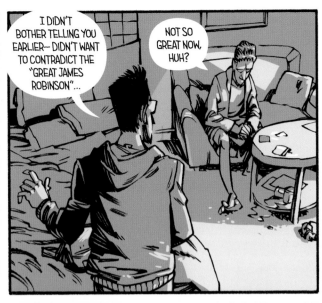

I DIDN'T BOTHER TELLING YOU EARLIER— DIDN'T WANT TO CONTRADICT THE "GREAT JAMES ROBINSON"...

NOT SO GREAT NOW, HUH?

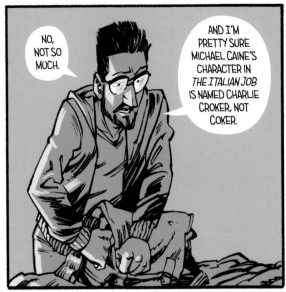

NO, NOT SO MUCH.

AND I'M PRETTY SURE MICHAEL CAINE'S CHARACTER IN *THE ITALIAN JOB* IS NAMED CHARLIE CROKER, NOT COKER.

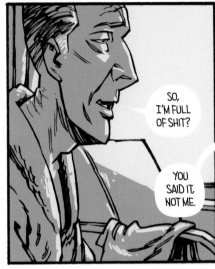

SO, I'M FULL OF SHIT?

YOU SAID IT, NOT ME.

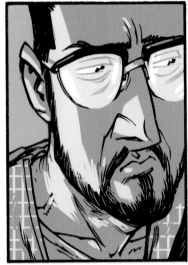

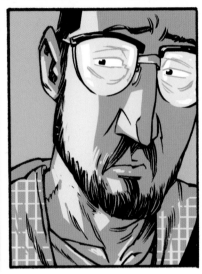

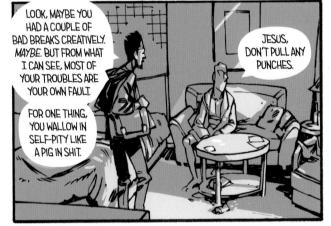

LOOK, MAYBE YOU HAD A COUPLE OF BAD BREAKS CREATIVELY. *MAYBE.* BUT FROM WHAT I CAN SEE, MOST OF YOUR TROUBLES ARE YOUR OWN FAULT.

FOR ONE THING, YOU WALLOW IN SELF-PITY LIKE A PIG IN SHIT.

JESUS, DON'T PULL ANY PUNCHES.

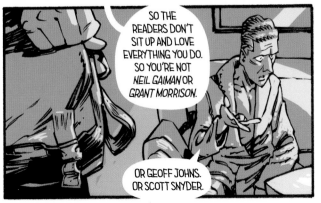

SO THE READERS DON'T SIT UP AND LOVE EVERYTHING YOU DO. SO YOU'RE NOT *NEIL GAIMAN* OR *GRANT MORRISON.*

OR GEOFF JOHNS. OR SCOTT SNYDER.

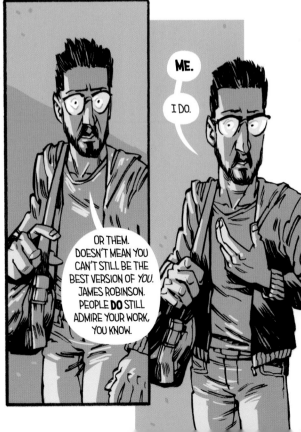

ME. I DO.

OR THEM. DOESN'T MEAN YOU CAN'T STILL BE THE BEST VERSION OF *YOU.* JAMES ROBINSON. PEOPLE **DO** STILL ADMIRE YOUR WORK, YOU KNOW.

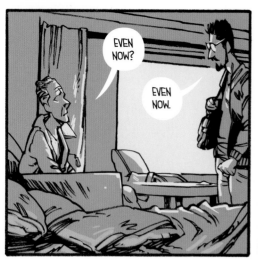

EVEN NOW?

EVEN NOW.

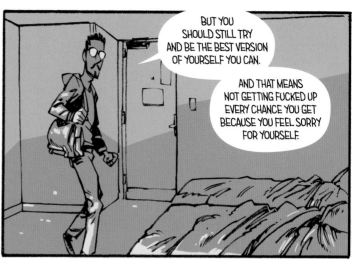

BUT YOU SHOULD STILL TRY AND BE THE BEST VERSION OF YOURSELF YOU CAN.

AND THAT MEANS NOT GETTING FUCKED UP EVERY CHANCE YOU GET BECAUSE YOU FEEL SORRY FOR YOURSELF.

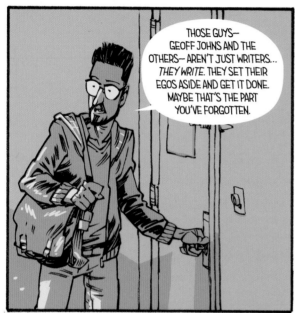

THOSE GUYS— GEOFF JOHNS AND THE OTHERS— AREN'T JUST WRITERS... *THEY WRITE.* THEY SET THEIR EGOS ASIDE AND GET IT DONE. MAYBE THAT'S THE PART YOU'VE FORGOTTEN.

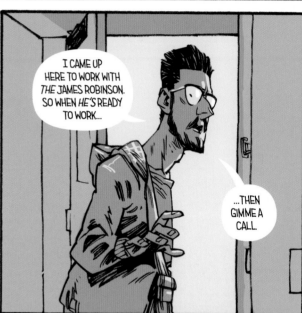

I CAME UP HERE TO WORK WITH *THE* JAMES ROBINSON. SO WHEN *HE'S* READY TO WORK...

...THEN GIMME A CALL.

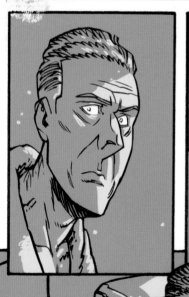

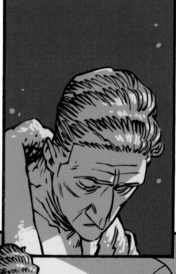

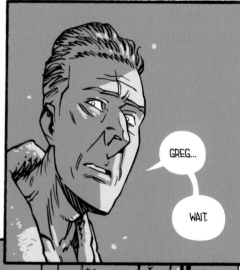

GREG...

WAIT.

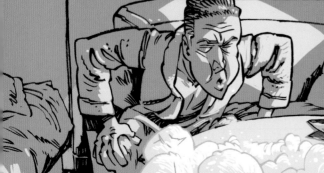

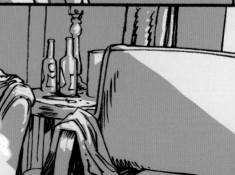

AIRBOY
JULY 10¢
COMICS

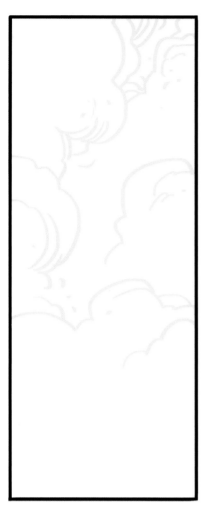

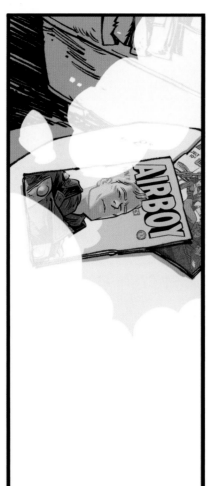

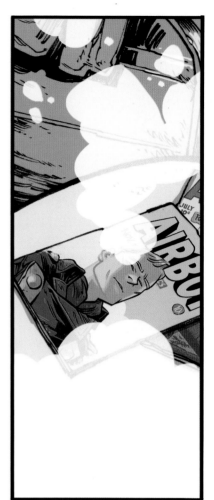

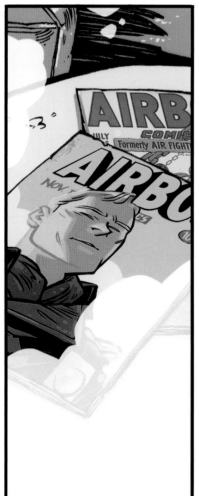

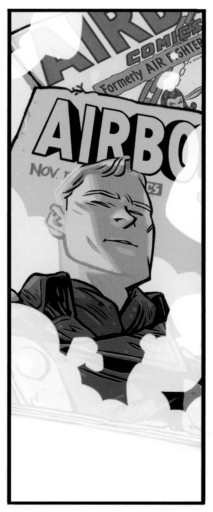

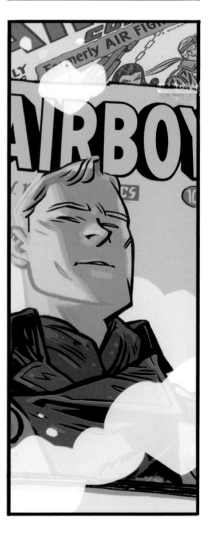

NOV.
10¢
THE END.

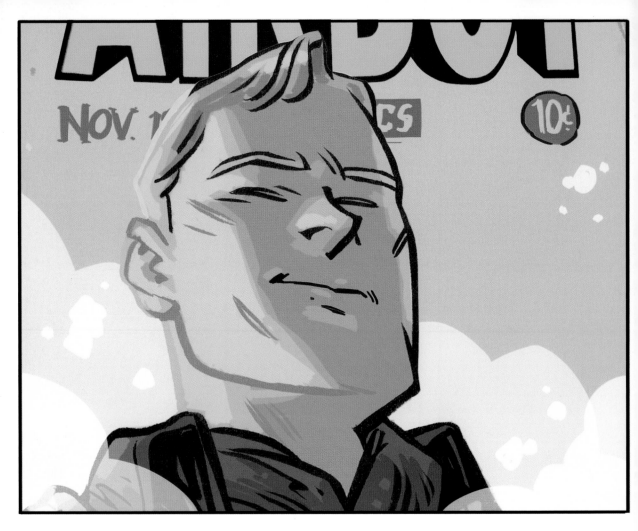

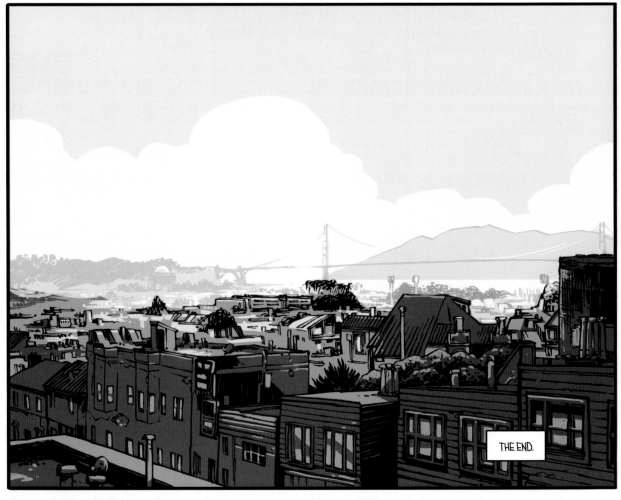

SO, THE FIRST QUESTION I'M ASKED BY PEOPLE ABOUT AIRBOY BY THOSE
WHO HAVE READ IT IS, "SO? DID YOU REALLY DO ALL THAT STUFF?
HOW MUCH OF IT IS TRUE?"

AND, THE ANSWER I ALWAYS GIVE IS "ALL OF IT, NONE OF IT,
MAKE UP YOUR OWN MIND."

I AM IMMENSELY PROUD OF THIS WORK, HOLDING IT AMONG THE BEST
THINGS I'VE EVER DONE. HOWEVER, I DO BELIEVE ARTISTIC VENTURES
WORK BEST WITH THE LEAST EXPLANATION. IT'S UP TO YOU NOW.

THANKS.

- JAMES ROBINSON

BEHIND THE SCENES WITH GREG

PAGES TWELVE/THIRTEEN.
SO EVERY ISSUE WERE GOING TO DO A DOUBLE PAGE SPREAD MONTAGE.
GREG.

WHAT THIS IS IS A MONTAGE OF JAMES AND GREG, DOING CRAZY SHIT,
EACH ISSUE APPERTAINING TO THE EVENTS OF THE MOMENT.

IN THIS MONTAGE WE SEE --

-- MULTIPLE IMAGES OF GREG AND JAMES DRINKING IN VARIOUS BAR
INTERIORS

-- ALSO MULTIPLE IMAGES OF JAMES AND GREG DOING COCAINE
TOGETHER ON THE ON THE BACK OF A CIGARETTE CASE THAT JAMES
HAS. FOR THIS THEY'RE IN ALLEYS AND IN THE BARS' BATHROOMS.
SOMETIMES BOTH OF MEN CRAMMED INTO THE BOOTH OF A BATHROOM
(WITH OUR POSES AWKWARD AND SOMEWHAT FUNNY) AS THEY BEND IN
TO SNORT A LINE WHILE THE OTHER HOLDS THE CIGARETTE CASE. AND
SOMETIME IN SINGLE BATHROOMS WITH A LOCK ON THE DOOR WHERE
THEIR ACTIONS CAN BE A BIT MORE OPEN.

-- THE TWO MEN STAGGERING DOWN DARK STREETS.

-- AN IMAGE OF THE PAIR OF THEM SIDE BY SIDE PISSING ON AN ALLEY
WALL.

-- LOTS OF NEON BAR SIGNS AND SUCH TOO, ALL OF THIS BLEEDING ONE
INTO THE NEXT.

-- SNORTING COKE --
GREG: So how do you know that guy that sold you this coke? He basically had a whole
       fucking pharmacy -- sniiiff.

JAMES: It's San Francisco. You meet people.

GREG: I lived here and I didn't "meet" people. Not like that weirdo.

TOP LEFT CORNER ① *SCORING*

JAMES: He's actually quite a gifted violinist.

GREG: Really?

JAMES: No.

JAMES: Enough questions. You're worst than a narc. Come on, it's Friday, let's party.

GREG: But I thought I was up here to work. That's the only reason my wife said it was
      okay.

JAMES: We will work, don't worry.

JAMES: Tomorrow.

-- GREG AND JAMES AT A BAR. JAMES IS SQUEEZING HIS NOSE, LIKE HE'S
GOT SOMETHING STUCK UP IT --

JAMES: Owwy. That charlie is stingy, boy.

GREG: Well it's made me sober again all of a sudden.

JAMES: Only one way to cure that...

HIDEOUT 2 panels

JAMES (CALLING TO BARTENDER): ...Two more!

-- SHOTS OF JAMES LEADING GREG IN AND OUT OF THIS OR THAT BAR --

JAMES: Come on, this place is too crowded.   *3 panels*

JAMES: Come on, this place is dead.

JAMES STANDING IN THE STREET, TENSING HIS STOMACH, BIDDING GREG
TO PUNCH IT.
Punch. Right in the gut. Go on. I can take it.   *1 panel*

JAMES HANDING GREG A PILL
JAMES: Here.

GREG: What's this?   *SPECS ② panels*

JAMES: I got some ecstasy when I bought the blow. The coke's speedy, this'll mellow
you out.

GREG: Err. Fuck it, what have I got to lose?

AT A BAR IN AMONG THE CROWD
JAMES: Where did you go?   ②

GREG: I didn't like that you paid for all the drugs, so I got us some coke too.

JAMES: Niiice. Fresh Charlie. What a gentleman.

BOURBON & BRANCH 2 panels

JAMES: Shall we avail ourselves of the bathroom?

JAMES OFFERS GREG A DIFFERENT PILL   *1 panel*

JAMES: Ever tried horse tranquilizer? You really should.

-- JAMES STANDING ON SOMEONE'S CAR RANTING AND RAVING. GREG IS
HORRIFIED --

   2 panels

JAMES: Maybe it's the name. Airboy.

JAMES: Maybe that's what's throwing me off. It's such a stupid fucking name.

GREG: Who's fucking car is that? Get down off it! Fuck.

BY THE TIME THE SCRIPT LANDED ON MY DESK, IT
WAS PRETTY WELL FORMED. BUT THAT DOESN'T MEAN IT WAS
FIGURED OUT.

TAKE THE "BENDER SPREAD", FOR INSTANCE. THE ORIGINAL
SCRIPT (LEFT) HAS ALL THE PANEL DESCRIPTIONS, AND STORY
BEATS, BUT NOT NECESSARILY IN THE RIGHT ORDER. SO THAT'S
WHERE I STARTED. BREAKING DOWN THE PIECES, AND
REORDERING THEM IN A WAY THAT MADE SENSE FOR
THE STORY.

I WANTED TO INCLUDE REAL LOCATIONS AND MOVE THROUGH
THE CITY ALONG A BELIEVABLE PATH. WE START UP AROUND
RUSSIAN HILL, HEAD THROUGH THE BROADWAY TUNNEL INTO
CHINATOWN AND NORTH BEACH, DOWN INTO THE TENDERLOIN,
AND END UP DEEP IN THE MISSION DISTRICT.

THE KEY (BELOW) IS WHAT KEPT EVERYTHING IN ORDER
AT THE TIME. NOW I CAN'T HARDLY MAKE ANY SENSE OF IT.

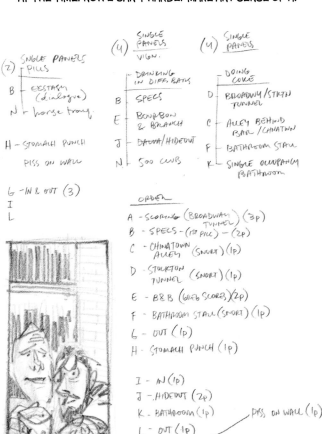

(2) SINGLE PANELS - PILLS
B - ECSTASY (dialogue)
N + horse tranq.

H - STOMACH PUNCH
PISS ON WALL

G - IN & OUT (3)
I
L

(4) SINGLE PANELS VIGN.
- DRINKING IN DIFF. BARS
B - SPECS
E - BOURBON & BRANCH
J - DACHA/HIDEOUT
N - 500 CLUB

(4) SINGLE PANELS
- DOING COKE
D - BROADWAY/STKTN TUNNEL
C - ALLEY BEHIND BAR/CHINATWN
F - BATHROOM STALL
K - SINGLE OCCUPANCY BOATHROOM

ORDER
A - SCORING (BROADWAY TUNNEL) (3p)
B - SPECS - (1st PILL) - (2p)
C - CHINATOWN ALLEY (SNORT) (1p)
D - STOCKTON TUNNEL (SNORT) (1p)
E - B&B (GREG SCORES) (2p)
F - BATHROOM STALL (SNORT) (1p)
G - OUT (1p)
H - STOMACH PUNCH (1p)
I - IN (1p)
J - HIDEOUT (2p)
K - BATHROOM (1p)   PISS ON WALL (1p)
L - OUT (1p)
M
N - 500 CLUB (HORSE TRANQ) (1p)
O - TOP OF CAR (2p)   = 21 panels

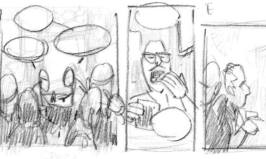

A THUMBNAIL WAS DONE FOR EACH PANEL OR MOMENT, AND THEN REARRANGED IN PHOTOSHOP UNTIL IT SEEMED COHERENT. I DIGITALLY SKETCHED OVER THE THUMBNAILS, TWEAKING AND FLIPPING THINGS AS I WENT. THIS WAS THE MOST COMPLICATED THING I'D EVER ATTEMPTED AT THE TIME, AND I REMEMBER FIGHTING WITH IT FOR DAYS. AND IT DIDN'T GET ANY EASIER WHEN I WAS DONE INKING. I STILL HAD TO FIGURE OUT HOW TO DISTINGUISH DIFFERENT LOCATIONS WITH THE LIMITED PALETTE WE'D ESTABLISHED FOR THIS PART OF THE BOOK. BUT NOBODY SAID THIS WOULD BE EASY...

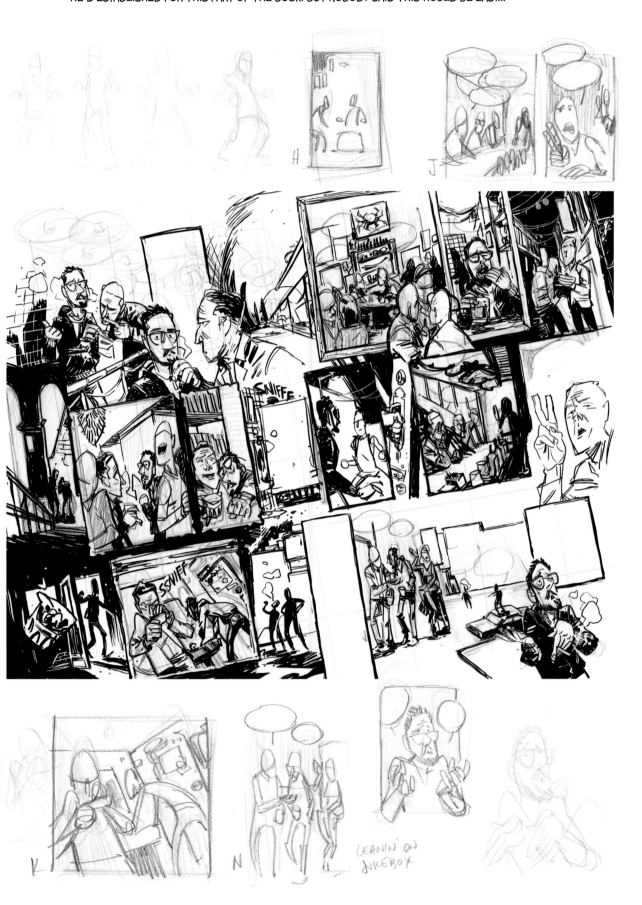

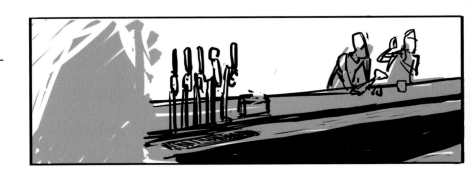

RIGHT - DIGITAL THUMBNAIL

BELOW :
A - FINISHED LINE ART
B - GREEN TONE
C - BLUE TONE ADDED
D - YELLOW OVERLAY

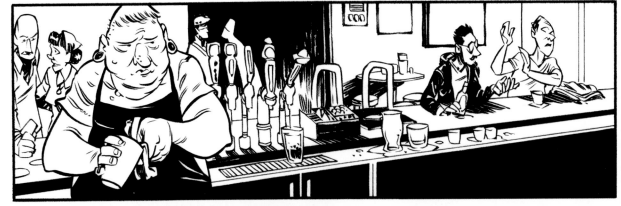

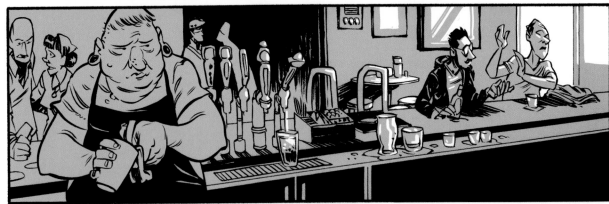

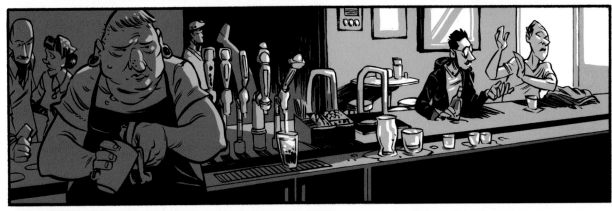

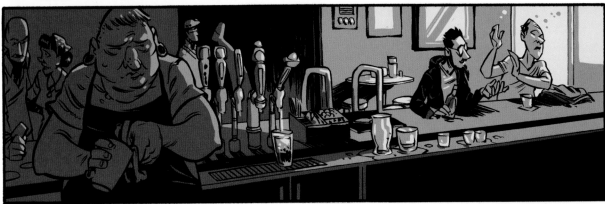

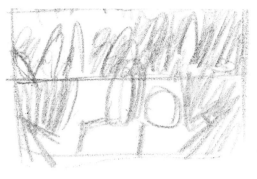

I LIKE TO BUILD LITTLE 3D MODELS (USING GOOGLE SKETCHUP) TO KEEP SCENERY AND PROPS CONSISTENT. USING MODELS ALSO LETS ME FOCUS ON POPULATING A SCENE RATHER THAN PERFECTING THE PERSPECTIVE.

AFTER ESTABLISHING THE BASIC BLOCKING IN THE THUMBNAIL (THOSE BLUE SCRIBBLES TO THE LEFT), I ASSEMBLED A MODEL, TOOK A SCREENGRAB OF THE BEST SHOT, AND PAINTED RIGHT OVER IT IN PHOTOSHOP. THAT ROUGH IS TRANSFERRED TO MY FINAL PAPER AND INKED.

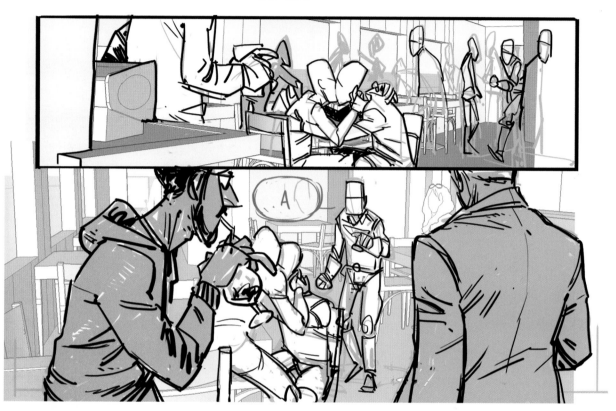

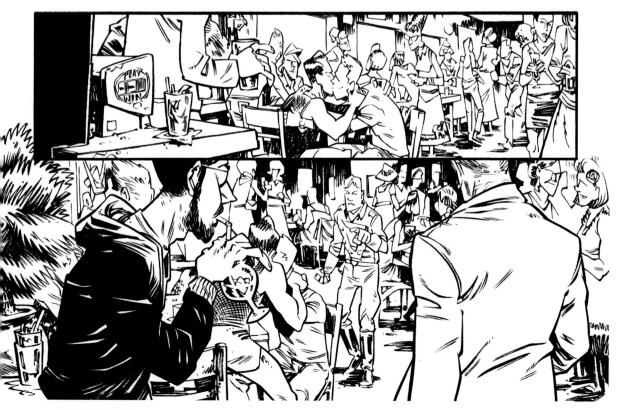

IRON ACE SKETCHES. THIS GUY WAS FUN TO FIGURE OUT.

PROGRESSION OF A
PANEL FROM THUMBNAIL
TO FINISHED ART.

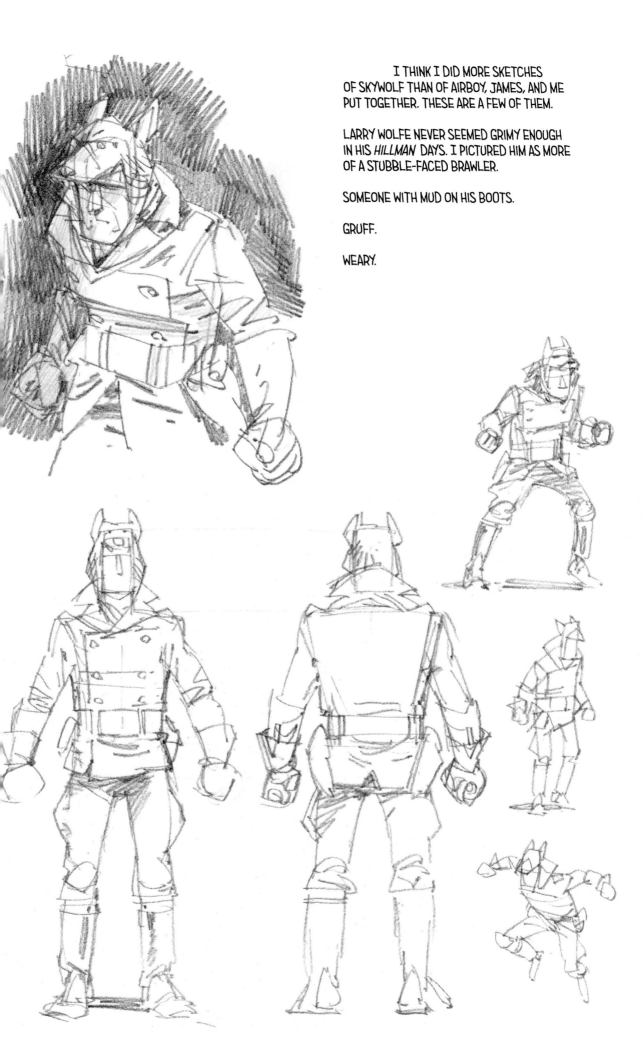

I THINK I DID MORE SKETCHES
OF SKYWOLF THAN OF AIRBOY, JAMES, AND ME
PUT TOGETHER. THESE ARE A FEW OF THEM.

LARRY WOLFE NEVER SEEMED GRIMY ENOUGH
IN HIS *HILLMAN* DAYS. I PICTURED HIM AS MORE
OF A STUBBLE-FACED BRAWLER.

SOMEONE WITH MUD ON HIS BOOTS.

GRUFF.

WEARY.

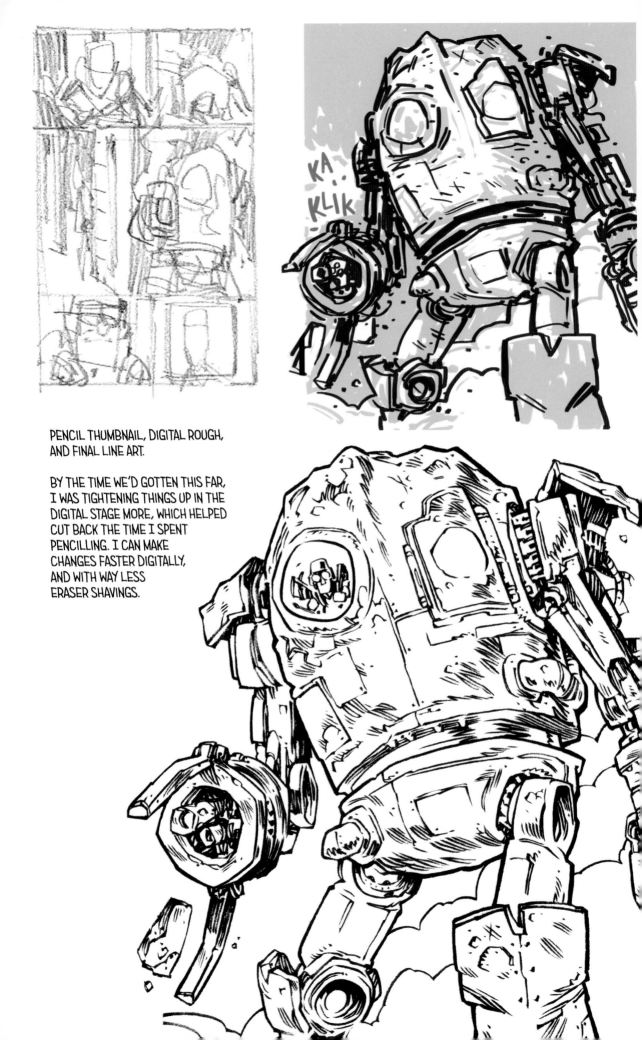

PENCIL THUMBNAIL, DIGITAL ROUGH, AND FINAL LINE ART.

BY THE TIME WE'D GOTTEN THIS FAR, I WAS TIGHTENING THINGS UP IN THE DIGITAL STAGE MORE, WHICH HELPED CUT BACK THE TIME I SPENT PENCILLING. I CAN MAKE CHANGES FASTER DIGITALLY, AND WITH WAY LESS ERASER SHAVINGS.

KA. KLIK

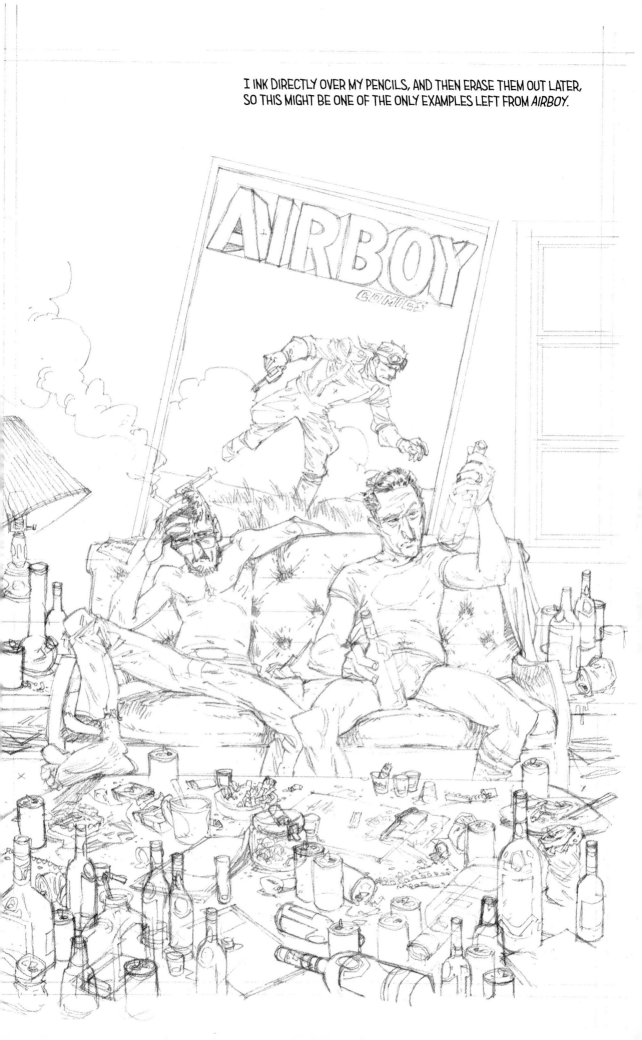

I INK DIRECTLY OVER MY PENCILS, AND THEN ERASE THEM OUT LATER, SO THIS MIGHT BE ONE OF THE ONLY EXAMPLES LEFT FROM *AIRBOY*.

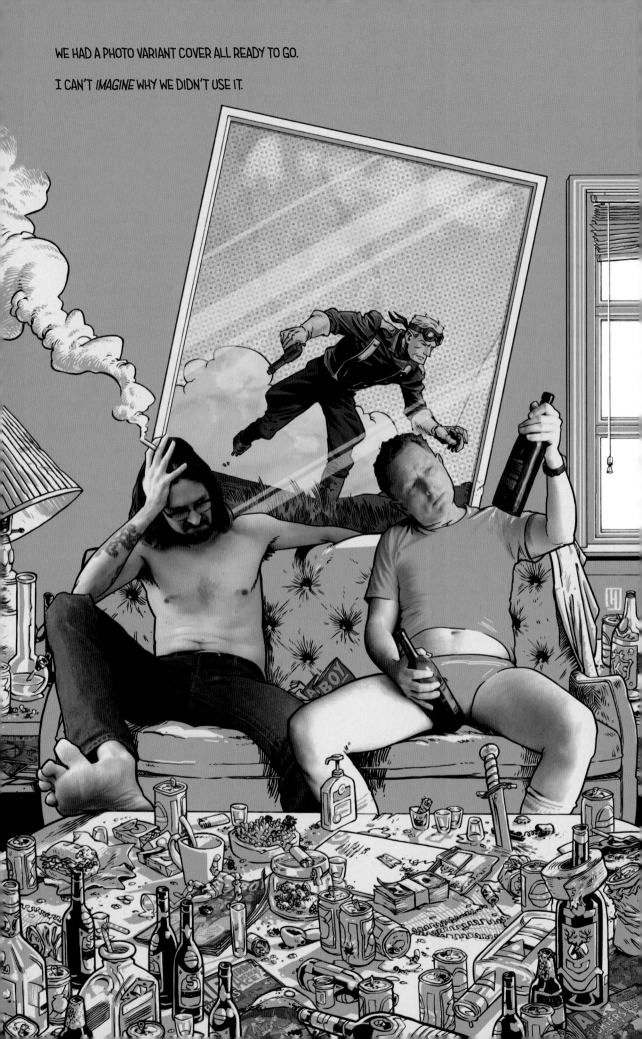

WE HAD A PHOTO VARIANT COVER ALL READY TO GO.

I CAN'T *IMAGINE* WHY WE DIDN'T USE IT.

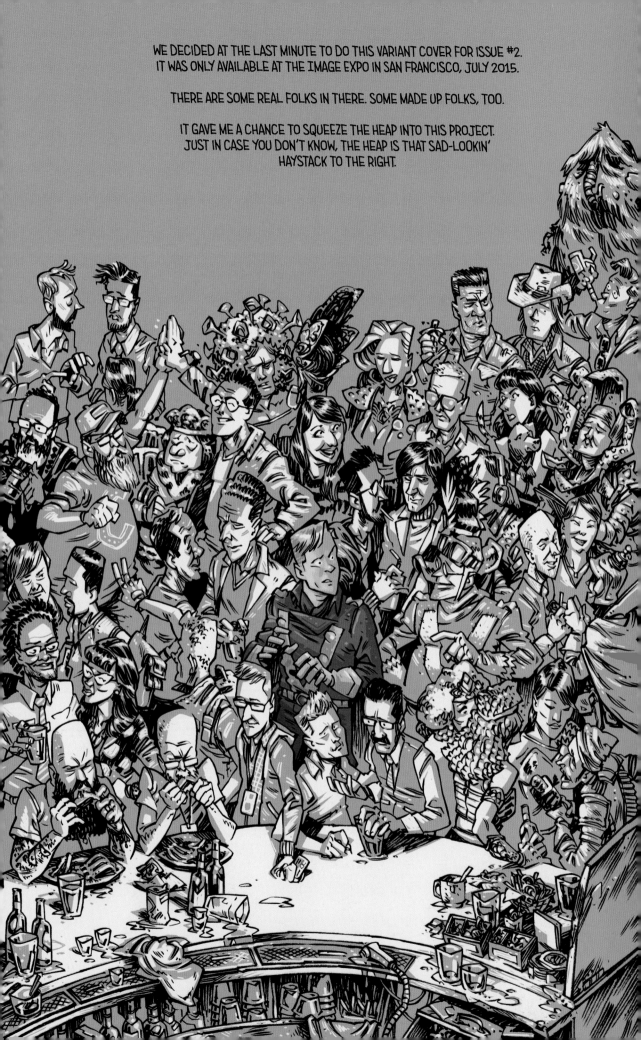

WE DECIDED AT THE LAST MINUTE TO DO THIS VARIANT COVER FOR ISSUE #2.
IT WAS ONLY AVAILABLE AT THE IMAGE EXPO IN SAN FRANCISCO, JULY 2015.

THERE ARE SOME REAL FOLKS IN THERE. SOME MADE UP FOLKS, TOO.

IT GAVE ME A CHANCE TO SQUEEZE THE HEAP INTO THIS PROJECT.
JUST IN CASE YOU DON'T KNOW, THE HEAP IS THAT SAD-LOOKIN'
HAYSTACK TO THE RIGHT.

JAMES ROBINSON HAS WRITTEN FOR MARVEL, DC AND DARK HORSE ON SOME OF THEIR MOST FAMOUS TITLES INCLUDING *SUPERMAN*, *FANTASTIC FOUR* AND *GRENDEL*. HE'S PERHAPS BEST KNOWN FOR HIS AWARD-WINNING RUNS ON *STARMAN* AND *LEAVE IT TO CHANCE*, AND WILL BE WORKING NEXT ON A NEW CREATOR OWNED SERIES, *HEAVEN*, AGAIN FOR IMAGE COMICS.

GREG HINKLE IS THE ARTIST AND CO-CREATOR OF *THE RATTLER* FOR IMAGE COMICS. HE LIVES IN SOUTHERN CALIFORNIA WITH HIS WIFE AND DOG. HE'S BOTH DIFFERENT AND SIMILAR TO HIS CHARACTER IN *AIRBOY*. HE'LL LEAVE YOU TO DECIDE WHAT'S REAL AND WHAT'S NOT.

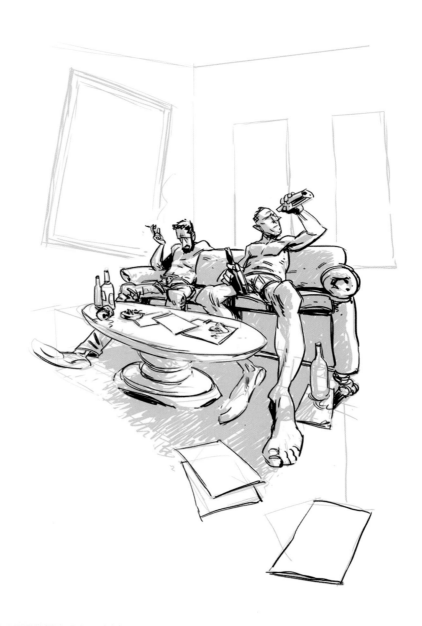